ONE-STRIKE

STOPPING POWER

D1523155

To Maynard

ONE-STRIKE

STOPPING POWER

How to Win Street Confrontations with Speed and Skill

Frank Albert

Paladin Press • Boulder, Colorado

One-Strike Stopping Power:
How to Win Street Confrontations with Speed and Skill
by Frank Albert

Copyright © 1993 by Frank Albert

ISBN 0-87364-714-9
Printed in the United States of America

Published by Paladin Press, a division of
Paladin Enterprises, Inc., P.O. Box 1307,
Boulder, Colorado 80306, USA.
(303) 443-7250

Direct inquires and/or orders to the above address.

Photo Credits:
Thomas Colley, Rhys Danylyshyn-Adams

Model Credits:
Steve Albrecht, Rhys Danylyshyn-Adams

Illustration Credits:
David Hodes, Mesa Valley Design, 8818 La Mesa Blvd., La Mesa, CA 92041.

Contents

INTRODUCTION 1

CHAPTER 1 -
Bad, Better, and
Best Target Zones 7

CHAPTER 2 -
Front and Side Fist Blows 33

CHAPTER 3 -
Chops, Palm Strikes, Ridge
Hands, and Finger Tears 53

CHAPTER 4 -
Elbow and Knee Blows 69

CHAPTER 5 -
Foot Chops,
Strikes, and Blows 83

CHAPTER 6 -
Pressure Point Nerves 107

Chapter 7 -
Movement and Positioning 117

CHAPTER 8 -
Hand, Wrist, and Finger
Strength Training 123

CHAPTER 9 -
Leg, Hip, and Foot
Strength Training 137

CHAPTER 10 -
The Dynamics of the Street 153

WARNING

Some of the self-defense techniques depicted in this book are extremely dangerous. This book is not meant to replace proper professional supervision and training by a certified self-defense instructor. Therefore, neither the author nor the publisher assume any responsibility for the use or misuse of information contained in this book. This book is for information purposes only!

"This is the law of the Yukon, that only the Strong shall thrive;
That surely the Weak shall perish, and only the Fit survive."
— Robert W. Service

Introduction

"When in doubt, duck."
—Malcolm S. Forbes

The specific title of this book is no accident. In a self-defense situation, it is possible and highly recommended that you try to disable your opponent with a single, well-placed blow. The street is not a safe fighting environment. It's not like a well-lit, well-padded gym or martial arts studio. Street people are not like your helpful workout partners who will "take it easy on you," let you practice a move slowly again and again until you get it right and not try to bite off your ear and stomp on your throat.

Street people usually have one of two goals: separate you from your wallet or separate you from your head. Some street people fight you to steal your money and others just because they enjoy violence. Either way, you could be in for a long night if one of these urban nuts gets the upper hand over you.

One-Strike Stopping Power will teach you to avoid missing money or missing teeth by getting in the first, fight-ending blow and then leaving. There is no dishonor in splitting after a violent confrontation. Nowhere does it say you have to stand around and wait for the cops or, worse, more of this person's friends to show up and come after you.

I can't count the number of times I've heard stories or seen firsthand where some regular Joe kicked the crap out of some street punk, only to be shot dead later by the wounded party or one of his pals. I am a firm believer in the old saying, "He who fights and runs away lives to fight another day."

There are no hard and fast rules on the street, save one: if you are confronted by someone intent on banging you around, you must get in the first knock, put him onto the concrete canvas, and place your feet into high gear.

There are no bells that signal the start of Round 1 in the street. There are no rest breaks, no penalty points for low blows, and, in fact, no fair-fighting rules at all. Whoever is left standing wins. It's as simple as that. Since the average street confrontation lasts about 20 to 45 seconds, the person who can disable and damage his opponent first will get out in one piece. Better this be you than the bad guy.

This book will give you some reasons why certain street-fighting techniques work and others won't. It's not designed to turn you into a boxer or a martial artist. Either of those disciplines takes years of dedicated practice for you to become skilled enough to use effectively. It's also not going to turn you into a trained killer, able to eat glass and spit nails. It will tell you what will work in a street encounter and what won't, with some exceptions. No one out there, bad guy or good, is a superhero, at least as far as I know. The size and shape of your enemy have something to do with your success rate, but not always. Your size, shape, conditioning level, and desire to win at all costs and not quit even if you get injured are all much more important to your personal success out in the streets.

I've seen too many guys who were built like apartment buildings get the royal hell knocked out of them by guys with pipe-stem arms and candy-cane legs. Do what works best for you and your body type. If you are lucky enough to have good genetics—strong legs, the ability to put on upper-body muscle, and a strong heart—you will obviously do better than most. However, if you aren't stacked like a Greek god, don't despair. Heart, technique, and guts have more to do with street victories than big arm muscles.

This book is easy to read and follow. Each chapter builds upon the others, and I review key concepts at intervals. The only way to improve your streetfighting abilities is to train, over and over again, until you know how to do the moves that will serve you best.

Studies of body motion and habit tell us that the average person needs to perform a muscle movement from 3,000 to 5,000 times before it becomes ingrained and locked into his or her memory banks. When you can react automatically, without stopping to think what to do or how to do it, you've reached that "muscle memory" stage, where the body takes over and leaves the mind behind.

This is also a visual book. It's easy enough to tell you about street confrontation attacks and defenses, but it's better to show you. The descriptive illustrations and photos should help you better understand the positions and the movements. The chapters are short, the language is clear, and the movements are based upon sound advice I've received from masterful streetfighters and what I've learned on my own. I've spent years working the streets, in martial arts studios, and in weight-lifting gyms, but I still have a lot to learn about my own body and how to use it most effectively against people who put harm in my way.

While I'm no master on the hows and whys of street violence, I have seen more and I know more than most so-called "experts." My experience in confrontational situations has taught me some valuable lessons. Some I learned the hard way—and I have the scars to prove it—and others I learned by dishing out healthy helpings of ass-whip myself.

As with most things in life, take what you can use, adapt it to your particular situation, and go to it when the chips are down. Read and learn with an open mind and improve upon the things that appeal to you.

Most martial arts teach various self-defense techniques to use against armed opponents. Unless you are a master martial artist, many of these techniques will not work well during an armed confrontation. In the safety of the studio, it's easy to believe that you can prevent slashing knife blows, disarm gun-toting assailants, or block overhead stick smashes with crossed wrists above your head. Real life tells us something different.

Fighting with an unarmed enemy is a scary, nerve-rattling event. Your adrenaline will pump like rocket fuel and you may barely be able to keep your body vertical because your legs are shaking so badly. Give your opponent a deadly weapon—from a screwdriver or a broom handle all the way up to an assault rifle—and you could be paralyzed by the fear of death. This is a normal response to such a situation. No matter how many times you hear some tough guy say, "Oh yeah? Well, I'd have grabbed that gun and kicked his ass!", don't believe it. Our fear of weapons and the pain, injury, or death they can deliver goes all the way back to our primeval caveman days.

There are no gun take-aways, knife sweep-aways, or stick blocks in this book. I've yet to learn a self-defense technique that will work when some hopped-up dope fiend is aiming a gun at your chest from a distance of 10 feet.

Don't mess with armed people. Nothing you own is worth more than your ability to breathe. I'll suggest some distraction techniques that might buy you some time to get away alive, but I will not advocate grappling for weapons if it's not an immediate life-or-death event. I know that more and more street hoods are arming themselves for their crimes. You will have to balance your desire to save your wallet or give up your life.

What would I do if I were accosted by an armed assailant and could not defend myself with a handgun? I'd give him my "mugger" wallet, which is actually a three-dollar spare I keep with my real one. This cheap wallet has about eight bucks in one-dollar bills in it, along with some phony-looking credit cards. I'd toss the wallet one way and run the other. Faced with the choice between a fleeing person and a wallet on the ground, what do you think the average street goon would do? Chase me down or go pick up the wallet before some other crook gets to it?

Throughout this book, I will use the terms "opponent," "enemy," "adversary," "attacker," "assailant," etc., interchangeably. Don't be confused by this; street people who wish to injure you—either as a result of a mugging or just for kicks—are all of these terms and more.

Further, in various places, I will point out certain "KEYS" to your understanding of the chapter. These keys should help you grasp the concept and use it to your best advantage.

Be consistent in your training, and focus your efforts toward doing the movements in an accurate and devastating fashion. *One-Strike Stopping Power* is a book that does what it says and says what it does. You can never be too aggressive in a real-life street encounter. Remember, this person wants to cause you as much pain as he probably feels in his own wretched life. Strike first, strike hard, and let him explain his actions to the cops or the emergency room doctors.

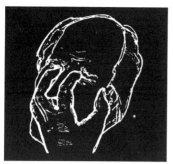

CHAPTER 1

Bad, Better, and Best Target Zones

"Go ahead, make my day."
—Clint Eastwood

Most streetfights start and finish with a looping right roundhouse punch to someone's head. And those that begin as pushing and shoving contests usually deteriorate into wrestling matches where both combatants end up on the ground.

This should tell you two things: the guy who gets in the first blow usually wins, and if you have to roll around with someone intent on cracking your skull, you probably will lose the battle.

Knowing how people brawl in the streets can go a long way toward helping you steer clear of their fists. Humans, as opposed to animals, usually fight forward, stepping toward the opponent and swinging away with a big punch to try and put the other guy down and out.

At the risk of sounding stupid, I'll ask you to consider this fact: when this alleged strategy works, it really works, and when it fails, it really fails. Knowing how to move laterally or backward, avoid the roundhouse to the jaw, and get in the first real fight-ending strike are the best things you can ever do in a street confrontation.

Those so-called "one-punch" fighters have rarely tangled with anyone who hits them back. The one who can get in the first shot, remain conscious if hit, take the most pain, and out-endure the other guy will stay on his feet and win by virtue of better survival skills. Rare is the fighter who moves laterally, gauges his enemy's strengths and weaknesses, and then goes about setting him on the ground in a quick, methodical fashion. That approach is what this book will teach you.

Move! Hit! Leave!

There are no polite Marquis of Queensbury rules in streetfights; you should do whatever it takes to win and survive. If you grew up in a neighborhood where crime and other associated urban problems were unheard of, then you may have a hard time convincing yourself that it's acceptable to fight "dirty." If you need someone to give you permission, I will. Now hear this: *it's okay to fight dirty!* Rest assured that the people who grew up in tough, inner-city war zones know about dirty fighting firsthand. They have seen it, done it, or had it laid upon them by other people who never read rule books or helped little old ladies across the street.

The human body is a wondrous thing. All those muscles, nerves, and tendons, mixed with healthy doses of fear-laced adrenaline, can turn you from a normal person into a ravaging maniac and then back into a normal person. The organ that allows you to shift from this one extreme to the other is the brain. Fortunately for you, your brain is infinitely better-equipped than the one belonging to the average street creature. His mental capacity has probably been damaged by assorted street drugs, copious quantities of cheap booze, and an assortment of blows to the head from other like-minded folks. Your capacity to think, reason, and make quick judgments can mean the difference between you or him riding on a gurney in an ambulance headed for the emergency room.

As a Confederate general said during the Civil War, "Get there firstest with the mostest." And so it goes with street confrontations. If you learn nothing else from this book, make sure this is carved into your memory banks: if you think the fight is about to happen, hit first and then leave the area. It's far better to be wrong and gone than right and out cold, out of money, or out of blood.

Follow the ancient Oriental martial arts idea of the "scholar-warrior." In days of old, the scholar-warrior was equally skilled at language, science, and numbers as he was at sword fighting, hand-to-hand combat, and horsemanship. These student-soldiers would work at such diverse topics as flower arranging and calligraphy, then go out and practice the death techniques that made them such fierce samurai combatants. While they strived to exhibit peaceful qualities, they would not hesitate to kill when the need arose.

Thanks to modern times, you don't have to follow this model so strictly. Your credo should be to avoid street confrontations but always settle them in your favor should they occur.

STREETFIGHTING RITUALS

Most street people start their fights with a sucker punch, a grab from behind, or a shove to the ground. If you can get in the first punch or kick and immediately disable your opponent, you will win the majority of street confrontations. A carefully placed punch to the "knockout" areas of the head, a hard kick to the abdomen, a strike to the testicles, or a kick or elbow to a knee joint will take the fire out of even an experienced street brawler. Many so-called "fighters" aren't used to getting hit back. In some cases, they are better at dishing out agony than absorbing it. Faced with a crippling dose of pain—something that immobilizes their thinking, breathing, and moving abilities—they will almost always throw in the towel.

Anytime you initiate a striking or kicking movement designed to stop your opponent or put him off his feet, remember to let simple physics work for you. Gravity is a tough law to break. I don't know anyone who has figured out how to suspend this apple-dropping decree. In a street confrontation, get some help from Sir Isaac Newton: let the ground rush up to meet your opponent's face, body, or limbs.

In the judo studio, I learned to protect my partner from harm and "guide" him as gently as possible to the mat. You don't need to heed this practice in the streets. Hit or kick your enemy and step back. If he falls, it's likely his head or face will reach the hard pavement, the curb edge, a nice soft brick wall, a parked car, a newspaper rack, or a convenient fire hydrant in order to prove the law of gravity correct. Let the ground do some damage for you. It adds more to your assaults without causing you to exert any extra effort.

THE B.E.A.T. MODEL

This book will teach you to follow a simple model, coined in an easy-to-remember acronym called B.E.A.T. Besides the word's obvious connection to fighting, it will teach you to focus on specific target strike points in order to disable the following areas:
B—Brain
E—Eyes
A—Abdomen
T—Testicles
Let's start at the top and work down.

Brain

We like to think that our brains are like small personal computers, whirring away solving problems and spitting out answers and actions for us to follow. While this image of the brain as a machine works in children's cartoons, in reality, the human brain is more like a floating bowl of gelatin wedged inside a coconut. Our gray cells give us the capacity to think, act, and reason, but for all the built-in complexities, the brain is still a very delicate instrument.

Even the slightest jarring sensation will shut down the mighty machine for a few seconds. Take a hard shot to the head and the brain will bounce up against the side of your skull, turn off, and fade to black. Welcome to the unpleasant land of unconsciousness.

Although your brain is covered by the eight thick bones of your skull, there are weak points and kinks in this armor-plated area. Under the right circumstances, it's easily struck, easily injured, and, unlike broken bones or bruises that heal, it can get ruined permanently.

Fortunately, most street people don't put this region to use very often. Let's just say it's not their largest or most-used organ.

With all this in mind, let's start by learning to strike the areas on the head that will cause unconsciousness in your opponent. This includes the jaw points, behind the ear, and the vulnerable sides of the neck. A sharp, well-placed blow to any of these will knock your opponent out. Elbow and fist blows to the temple, back of the neck, and throat also will "turn out the lights."

THE SIDE OF THE JAW MAKES AN EXCELLENT KNOCKOUT PUNCH TARGET.

Punches to the head area are the most common fighting tactic because it's such an instinctive response for most people. It's much easier and faster to get your fist into his face. But fists to the head are not the only way to start and end streetfights. Since I feel this book is the "Thinking Man's

Guide to Streetfighting," we won't always do what our enemies expect.

Learn and memorize the brain's points of unconsciousness:

• *The sides of the jaw.* This area is a favorite of boxers and martial artists. A solid punch, kick, or elbow shot to this area—about 3 inches up from the point of the jaw—will send your enemy crashing to the ground in a haze of darkness. In physiological terms, a hard jaw blow breaks the small bones leading back to the jaw joint itself. This damage sends a "lights-out" signal to the brain.

Similarly, a straight blow to the point of the jaw also will cause the same result by breaking the small bones at the base of the jaw. Many streetfighters and even experienced martial artists get knocked out in this manner because, during a conflict, they may leave their mouths open to draw in more air. Fighting with an open mouth is an invitation to a broken jaw or unconsciousness. Learn to breathe through your clenched teeth and leave the heavy huffing and puffing and "kiai" yells back where you train.

• *The temple and side of the head.* A hard punch, kick, or elbow blow to this bony area causes the internal bowl of gelatin known as the brain to splash against the side of the coconut known as the head. Hitting this target area is especially effective if the opponent is lung-

A HARD BACKFIST SHOT TO THE TEMPLE CAN REALLY RATTLE YOUR OPPONENT'S BRAIN.

ing toward you or moving away. The speed of your fists or feet and the speed of his moving head add up to high-velocity pain.

• *The ear area.* A favorite with organized crime members. Attacking the ear region can bring on three unique events: most people don't expect to be injured here, so they can become disoriented; the pain is intense, mind-numbing, and has a certain psychological and internal "intrusiveness" about it; and, lastly, no one likes to be deafened during a fight.

Open palm slaps or closed fist blows to one or both ear holes can cause immediate deafness by rupturing the ear drums or even death by internal bleeding if some other physiological trauma factors come into play. In any instance, on-target ear blows will send shock waves deep into the brain. The pain is intense and excruciating and it can bring on a tremendous desire in your enemy to crawl into a hole and wait for the loud thumping sensation to go away.

• *Portions of the neck and back of the head.* A sharp fist blow or palm chopping movement to the side of the neck can generate powerful shock waves into your opponent's entire upper torso. Striking the neck muscles of an attacker who is unprepared can cause an involuntary flinching motion that closes his eyes, hunches his shoulders, or bends him over.

Attacking the brain via the head offers you one of the

AN OPEN PALM STRIKE TO THE EAR DEAFENS, DISABLES, AND DOWNS YOUR ATTACKER.

best chances of knock-out success. Most fights start and end here, with the winner able to dish out the most punches and incapacitate his opponent through blood, pain, and shock. In general, it also helps to see the head in two ways: as an entire target itself and as an area filled with a number of specific targets, like the nose and throat. Learning to hit these areas with the weapons at your disposal—fists, chops, palm strikes, elbows, headbutts, knees, and feet—is the best way to follow the Golden Rule: hit them before they hit you, then get out.

Headbutts

This one is popular in Arnold Schwartzenegger movies and for good reason—it works. Obviously, the headbutt movement is a close-quarters attack. And because your head bends in a number of different directions, including the ever-popular forward and backward, you can strike out at your assailant if he

grabs you from the front or seizes you from behind. Just remember an important safety tip: use the hardest parts of your head—the top and forehead areas—to smash the softest parts of his face, usually the nose, mouth, and eye sockets.

Banging your bony head against his bony head may get you out of his grasp and able to finish the fight, but it probably will send you away bleeding. The fore-

USE THE BASE OF YOUR CLOSED FIST TO STUN THE NERVES AND ARTERIES IN THE SIDE OF HIS NECK.

head is filled with tiny capillaries and blood vessels that sit close to the surface of the skin and rupture easily.

And don't just rely on one head-butting movement to incapacitate your enemy. Let your head pound back and forth like a jackhammer until he falls clear. Let him pay for the nose job.

IF YOUR ATTACKER GRABS YOU FROM THE FRONT, USE YOUR FOREHEAD LIKE A BATTERING RAM AGAINST HIS FACE.

The Nose
A strike to the nose has several repercussions attached to it. While some nose shots may stun the opponent and disorient him, others will cause his nose to break. As anyone who has ever broken his nose will tell you, it can be excruciat-

THE BACK OF YOUR HEAD IS EVEN TOUGHER THAN THE FRONT.

ingly painful. There is relatively soft cartilage tissue inside here; it doesn't take much force to crush it beyond repair. Even a glancing nose strike (notice I don't call them nose "blows" to avoid the obvious symbolism) will surely cause the nose area to rupture, swell, and probably bleed profusely.

Further, the sight of his own blood may cause several different reactions in your enemy. He may fall to the ground in shock and agony, he may become confused and flee, or he may become enraged and really come after you. Be prepared for all of these things, none of them, or combinations of the three.

For some people, seeing their own blood causes an adrenaline rush which may give them superhuman energy, endurance, or unequalled strength. In others, it may remind them of their limits, bring up images of their terrible childhood, remind them of their mortality, or put them into body-wrenching shock. While none of these should concern you, always remember that people are like animals and will respond in an animal-like "fight or flight" fashion.

KEY: Here's something important to keep in mind if you choose to strike the nose. If your opponent uses any drugs by inhaling them, such as cocaine or methamphetamine, his internal nasal passages will already be red, raw, and angry from all of that tissue-burning dope. Just tapping the nose of a

A STRAIGHT PUNCH TO THE NOSE CAN BRING TEARS, BLOOD, AND PAIN.

chronic snorter can bring tears to his eyes and gushing blood into his hands and face. Imagine how good you will feel if you land an accurate, powerful shot to this sensitive area.

A well-executed nose strike will certainly cause pain, possibly cause bleeding, and may even bring on tears from your opponent. Use this valuable disorientation time to strike other sites or to get out of the area. In target terms, just think of the nose as the "testicles of the head."

Throat and Neck

Hitting the throat is like eating a walnut. You have to work hard to get at the "meat," but once you do, it's very satisfying. Since your adversary will commonly protect his throat with his chin and shoulders, you need to get access to it by moving his head. You can do this by hitting him in a target area like the ear and attacking the throat as soon as he reacts to the pain. Or you

can grab the hair at the back of his head and pull it sharply away from you. This brings the delicate throat area into your attacking domain.

It doesn't take much to do serious and even fatal damage to the throat. It is not the purpose of this book to tell you how to kill people. However, the law says you have the right to defend your life if provoked by someone who wishes to injure you.

USE HIS HAIR AS A "HANDLE" TO GET TO THIS VULNERABLE SPOT.

Use your fist, the points of your fingers, or your elbow to strike this region and then quickly let go. It's hard to fight back if you can't breathe.

Like the bony skull, the neck is a "hard" target area. Even the best street and studio fighters have a hard time hitting the neck with enough accuracy and force to put an opponent down. Some people with an athletic background (weight lifters, wrestlers, boxers, and martial artists) may have such thick neck muscle "cords" that you just can't hit them there and expect to do much damage.

KEY: Besides the obvious discussions about where and how to hit your enemy, this book will spend time talking about people and places you should avoid and how to recognize them. If you see someone who has well-developed forearms, heavily muscled thighs, and a solid set of "traps" (trapezius muscles joining the neck-shoulder area), be very wary.

When I see this kind of build on a person, I know he has spent many hours lifting huge quantities of weights in a prison or a gym somewhere. This build is unique to power lifters and bodybuilders, who are not usually found in streetfighting environs. However, this depiction should send you a "be careful" message. Thick neck, arm, and leg muscles make for a harder target. You may have to rethink your strategy should you have to fight one of these people.

The Eyes

The muscles in and around our eyes are some of the smallest in our bodies. As an organ, the eye is also one of the most sensitive we have. It reacts strongly to light, pressure, and, in our case, the presence of foreign objects, like fingers and thumbs.

A well-placed eye shot stabbed into one or both eyes can stop any fight in seconds. Even the biggest guy in town will quit what he is doing (or plans to do to you) and try to cover his wounded socket with his hands. Any type of blindness scares people. It's a primitive instinct to protect our eyes from harm. A blinded prehistoric caveman could not hunt or protect his family from animals or other cavemen.

Eye shots cause immediate pain, tearing, swelling, redness, blurred vision, or even unconsciousness. One or more of these helpful reactions will give you enough time to finish the confrontation and get away. An episode of blindness, even for a short period, is disorienting, frightening, and may cause your enemy to bend over, back away, and howl in pain as you finish the fight or retreat from the scene.

Best of all, two- and four-finger eye shots, thumb "flick" shots, and spear hands to the face require little training (total accuracy is the only requirement), little force, and absolutely no special equipment. Old ladies, small children, and even the most passive person could bring a hulking idiot to his knees with a single, hard application to an eye.

If, despite your best efforts to poke your enemy's eyeballs

back into his skull, the fight looks like it will continue, simply move to this person's real "blind side" and choose another weapon in your arsenal to finish the encounter. He'll never see that last punch or kick until it's too late.

Don't think that sunglasses or eyeglasses will protect your opponent from eye and thumb shots. You can rip away

THINK OF YOUR FINGERS AS IF THEY WERE SHARP SWORDS AND DIG THEM INTO HIS EYES.

these plastic or glass barriers with one

hand while you dig in with the other. Or simply push up under the glasses and into the eyes.

Abdomen

Most people, on the streets or otherwise, are soft-bellied and weak. Their solar plexus and lower abdominal regions offer inviting and debilitating targets. A sharp blow to the abdomen can cause an opponent to stop breathing temporarily. It also can cause fight-ending ruptures to the soft organs inside. Few people will not want to continue a confrontation after receiving such a blow.

Street people in particular are notorious for their poor eating habits and physical condition. Eating junk food fortified with drugs or alcohol does little to strengthen the abdominal region. As such, this is one of the most vulnerable points on their poison-filled carcasses. Many of these predatory folks are either slightly undernourished or cursed with an inviting "beer gut" that makes a safe, useful striking point.

Experienced martial artists know from training and sparring experience that the body's center of gravity sits at a point about 2 inches directly below the navel. This site—known in Oriental martial arts literature and folklore as the "chi" point—is extremely vulnerable to injury or distress.

PUNCH THE ABDOMEN BY DRIVING FORWARD WITH YOUR BODY WEIGHT.

Martial artists, boxers, and other experienced fighters will go to great lengths to both protect this area on their bodies and attack it on their opponent's.

The solar plexus, the diaphragm, and the soft intestinal regions are perfect recipients for hard shots. A single well-placed strike to any area around the navel can break ribs, rupture organs, and cause massive internal bleeding. If you doubt this, recall that our most famous escape artist, Harry Houdini, died from the pain of a ruptured appendix after receiving an abdominal blow from one of his "fans." This person was anxious to see if he could administer a stomach punch that Houdini could not withstand. He did and Houdini couldn't.

Like a blow to the head, an injury to the abdomen can knock your enemy off his feet and out cold. A simple tap to the gut won't do much. Like with anything taught in these pages, you'll need to put every ounce of energy and strength into the movement, be it a kick or punch. You must drive *through* the target, seeking to touch a point 3 feet past your opponent's stomach. By using your body weight and the torquing power of your hips, twist your punches or hammer your kick into his abdominal area hard, fast, and up toward the sky. Go up on your toes if you can. Imagine you are reaching completely through the oppo-

PUNCHING BELOW THE NAVEL WILL HIT HIS ENERGY-DRAINING "CHI" POINT.

nent's physical body, to a place completely

on the other side of him. Anything less than your best effort will not help you win.

KEY: Punching through your target is critical, but knowing how and when to *retract* your punch is equally important. Don't let your arms (or legs) just hang out there.

And just like the eye shot that bends your opponent over, you can follow an abdominal strike with another technique when your opponent is holding his belly and gasping for precious oxygen. In some cases, you can simply push him over like a spinning bowling pin. It's very difficult to think of anything other than breathing when you've had the "wind" knocked royally out of you.

The Testicles

No secret here. Few opponents can stand even a glancing blow to this vulnerable area. In the right circumstances, a hard strike from a knee, foot, or fist will cause ruptures, unconsciousness, or even death by shock or severe internal bleeding. I know two friends who needed emergency surgery to remove ruptured testicles after street confrontations. This is an exceedingly unprotected region of the male body.

KEY: The membrane that makes up the testicular sack itself is very thin and delicate, making it a prime target for grabbing, pulling, lifting, and tearing-type strikes. You only have to catch part of the sack and pull a few inches to create pain worthy of fireworks on the Fourth of July.

Since the testicle area is a low target, you can use a variety of attacking techniques to strike it:
• *Hammer fist.* Best used when you are slightly turned away from the enemy and he is coming toward you. Turn sideways, bend slightly at the waist, let your elbow socket extend out to its fullest, and hit the testicle area with your fist

A WELL-PLACED HAMMER
FIST WILL END THE FIGHT.

like it's a small punching bag.

• *Full front or side fist.* This move can be a lifesaver should you find yourself knocked to the ground with your attacker coming straight toward you. Just reach up and punch this area just as if it were the head or abdomen.

• *Front ridge hand chop.* A good close-quarter "flicking" movement. Imagine that the top or "ridge" part of your hand is like a snake. Tuck your thumb to the side of your palm, let this bony area flick out and uncoil into the testicle target, and then whip it back again.

• *Front snap kick (top of foot).* A perfect straight-on movement. Pull your knee up to your waist, aim

IF YOU SHOULD END UP BELOW YOUR AT-
TACKER, LASH OUT WITH A FRONT FIST PUNCH.

the top flat part of your foot at the target, and snap the kick out and back.

• *Scoop kick.* Just like the snap kick, except this time you curl your toes toward the sky for a scooping "hook" effect.

• *Rear kick.* Turn your back on your opponent, bend slightly at the waist, pull your knee close to your body, point your

THE BONY "RIDGE" ALONG THE TOP OF YOUR HAND WILL FEEL LIKE A 2X4 TO YOUR ASSAILANT.

toes toward the ground, and drive the heel of your foot into his testicles. This kicking move is excellent for an enemy who's chasing you. Stop and let him catch the heel of your foot.

The subject of testicle strikes is common to most women's self-defense classes. The course instructor usually

ANOTHER FIGHT ENDER, THE FRONT SNAP KICK IS EASY AND QUICK.

NOTICE THAT WITH THE FRONT SCOOP KICK, YOU PULL YOUR FOOT UP AND BACK.

gives a speech that sounds like this: "Ladies, whenever you're grabbed, assaulted, or harassed, go for the groin. A healthy kick to the private parts will bring down even the meanest, toughest mugger or rapist."

This sounds like good advice, and in most cases, it works. But I'm here to tell you from personal, painful experience that it's not always true. A "nut shot" will *not* always stop an attacker. As hard as this is to imagine, keep in mind that most longtime street hoods are continually under the influence of the mind-numbing chemicals found inside alcohol or drugs. Mix a snootful of liquor, methamphetamine, or cocaine

THE REAR KICK IS GREAT FOR PUTTING YOU IN THE BEST POSITION TO STRIKE AND LEAVE.

with large amounts of his adrenaline and you've created an effective painkiller.

Interviews with convicted rapists have uncovered a frightening phenomenon: some of them don't feel testicle strikes until hours after the incident is over. The booze, dope, and adrenaline served to mask the pain. They were able to take a crushing kick to the groin and still complete their attack, hardly pausing to feel the pain or injury. This is not to say they didn't feel it later or the strike did not injure them in some way, but only that a simple testicle attack did not stop them. I'll admit these are rare cases, but there are people floating around out there who are literally impervious to pain. Anyone taking the powerful painkilling hallucinogen PCP will not even feel the pain of broken bones or gunshot or stab wounds until many hours later.

The phrase "go for the jewels" should not be carved into stone. Like the other places in the B.E.A.T. model, it's merely another target. Hit hard there and get out of the way. You may need to avoid your opponent's falling torso or you may need to split because he will not stop even when you've given him your best nut shot.

KEY. Keep this in mind at all times—if a specific punch, kick, or striking technique fails to end the confrontation, do something else, and fast!

TARGETS TO AVOID

Now that the B.E.A.T. model has taught you where to hit, let's look at some places you should definitely avoid. In this discussion of acceptable target areas, keep this rule forever in mind: punch or kick with your hard objects (fists and feet) to your opponent's soft ones (nothing bony). Solid punches or kicks to the abdomen illustrate this point well. Sickly punches to the bony areas of the forehead or the top of the head will neither stop your enemy nor do anything but loads of damage

HITTING THE TOP OF HIS HEAD WITH YOUR
FIST ONLY HELPS HIM BY HURTING YOU.

to your multiboned and fragile hands.

Where not to hit: any area you might miss, or get hit in return, or be injured during the struggle. Avoid bony regions, heavily muscled body parts, or areas covered by big hats, thick coats, or other clothing that might protect the enemy's target zone. Smacking someone in the forehead with your fist probably will only annoy him and ruin your chances to ever play the piano correctly. You can spend hours hitting some "buffed out" muscleheads in places they won't even feel. Wailing away against fleshy chest, shoulder, and arm regions won't even raise a bruise on some of these folks.

Target areas work best where you can place something hard (your coiled fists, whipping feet, or snapping elbows) into something soft on your enemy (his nose, eyes, throat, abdomen, testicles, etc.) Two hard objects coming together (fist to head bone, foot to thigh muscle) usually cause more damage to the "hitter" than the "hittee." Hit his soft spots hard. It's one thing for you to win the fight and quite another for you to win and carry around a plaster case for six weeks.

MAKING ADJUSTMENTS

If this were a perfect world, each of the hand techniques

I've discussed would work flawlessly each time you applied them. Your hand positions would be ever so solid, you would always strike with power and accuracy, and your enemies would drop to the ground as if they fell from a high cliff. In a perfect fighting environment, everything you tried would work correctly and you would escape each encounter without a scratch.

This is not a perfect world. There is no such thing as a perfect fighting situation. Things happen. Problems arise, and your best laid plans can fail before you even try to put them to use. Punches can miss, hand strikes can wave at the air or glance off their targets, and your opponent can refuse to cooperate and not go down after you fire off the first blow.

So what do you do to counter the imperfect happenings in our imperfect world? You improvise, you keep going, you try something else, and you fight harder.

One of the main problems I see with martial artists and fighters who are locked into one or two "favorite" moves is that when these so-called flawless techniques fail—and they do fail on occasion—the fighter is left in the lurch. Sometimes the fighter will get so bamboozled because of a "broken" technique that all common sense and, worse yet, survival instincts fly out the window. Instead of backing up, spitting in their palms and saying, "Well, the fight has *really* begun," too many of these folks lose their train of thought and can't continue effectively.

Anytime your game plan gets interrupted, switch to something else. If one punch has failed, change to another and hit harder! If your attacker does everything you don't want him to do, go with his flow, readjust yourself, and let him have it again. Don't fall in love with one hand technique to the exclusion of all others. Be flexible and know enough about each technique to use it when others have failed you.

If front fist punches don't seem to be doing anything for you, be ready to change hand positions to hammer fists quickly and keep going. Rely on combinations to help you

BAD, BETTER, AND BEST TARGET ZONES

put your assailant down and out. Hit once, hit twice, and hit three times in quick succession. Street fighting is like eating donuts: if one is good, then two and three are better. Hit! Hit! Hit! Use your left and right hands separately and then in conjunction as combination punches.

Make sure you step through with your punches. Hit the area 3 feet past your opponent's B.E.A.T. model zones. Don't stay static; keep moving. A boxer who tries to go toe-to-toe with his opponent may lose the fight even if he is bigger, stronger, or technically superior. Move away from his trouble and move in to strike him. Don't reverse these two! Moving in to get hit and moving out of target range to swing at the air is the best way to visit your local hospital.

Learn to fight forward, laterally, and backward, punching as you go in and out. Many a fight has ended after the superior fighter punched as he moved away from trouble. There is no shame in backing up, as long as you use your enemy's forward movement as an aid to your assault.

BODY QUADRANTS

I've already mentioned that street problems are quite stressful and can cause your mind and body to play nasty tricks on each other. With a pounding heart and fear pervading your brain, you can lose track of time, shapes, and distance. It's a strange paradox that when you need your body most, it has a noticeable tendency to fade out on you.

Be aware and ready for the symptoms of paralyzing alarm, acute tunnel vision, and a bad case of "noodle" arms and "licorice" legs. During times like these, it may be hard to concentrate on your B.E.A.T. model targets. Therefore it often helps to divide the front and back of your attacker's body into three quadrants: upper, middle, and lower.

With the upper-facing targets, you'll want to aim your fist blows at his nose, eye sockets, throat, side of his neck, side of his jaws, and temple. Keep the "hard to soft" connection in mind at all times: don't slam your bony hands against his bony areas; instead, use your hard fighting tools against his softest targets.

For the middle-facing targets, punch out and into his heart, ribs, abdomen, and internal organs.

Lower-facing targets include the testicles and, to a lesser extent, your attacker's load-bearing joints like the knees, ankles, and shin bones.

To capitalize on the rare chance that you may be able to get behind your assailant, keep these upper, middle, and lower targets in mind: the back of his neck, his ear holes, his rib sides near the arm pits, his kidneys and lower back, and even the testicle sack, which you can easily attack with a well-placed hammer fist.

GETTING BEHIND YOUR OPPONENT

Before you can attack your enemy's rear targets, you'll have to devise a rapid way to get behind him. How successful you are at this depends upon a number of factors, including your attacker's relative level of sobriety, his size, what kind of clothing he's wearing, your footing, the conditions of the street where the confrontation is taking place, and the amount of room you have to maneuver.

If your assailant is stone drunk or high on heroin, he may be easy to shove around and get behind. However if he has smoked PCP or rock cocaine or snorted methamphetamine, he may be too flighty to move.

His size and shape also will influence if and how you attack him from behind. If he is large and squatty, he may be harder to move than if he is tall and thin. Further, if he's wearing many layers of bulky clothing, it may be either difficult or easy to grab him and spin him around.

If you're boxed in by buildings, walls, or other impediments like cars and mailboxes, or if you're standing on broken, icy, or muddy ground, try to move as little as possible when you strike. Any encounter with loose gravel, curb abutments, or even dog droppings could put you on your back. Being on the ground could signal the start of a long and painful day for you, especially if your attacker has got some hard-toed friends in the area.

KEY: One of the best ways to get behind your foe is by distracting him first. If you're in low light or near darkness, so much the better. You can scream at him, clap your hands, or yell wildly and wave your arms in the air. All of these movements do two things: they make him stop and think about your sanity level—even for a second—and they give you more time to move behind him and attack.

Once you start your initial rear move, do it quickly, grabbing his jacket, hat, hair, or anything that might look like a handle on his body. Once you get behind, grab and shove his head or one of his shoulders down toward the pavement. Try to buckle his knee by kicking at the back of this fragile joint. Stomp on his Achilles tendon above his heel as you pull him by the coat to the hard ground.

While you won't usually begin your attack from the rear, in some unusual situations you may need to know how to attack specific targets from behind. Strike between his legs from behind and you'll catch his testicles. Batter his locked knee joints with hard kicks and you'll knock him down. Step hard on his ankles and calves as you pull him off balance.

CHAPTER 2

Front and Side Fist Blows

"Answer violence with violence!"
—Juan Peron

Too much of what we think we know about the subject of streetfighting has come from television and the movies. As entertaining as those mediums may be, they fail to show the realities of real street confrontations. On the screen, the talented fighter brawls with his opponent, skillfully blocking his blows, absorbing the occasional brutal punch that gets through, and dishing out plenty of old-fashioned pain with his dukes.

What TV and the movies fail to capture is how difficult streetfighting really is, to wit:

• In most encounters, you must hit a moving target.

• Your opponent is not a stuntman but rather probably someone under the influence of pain-masking drugs or alcohol.

• The conditions—lighting, footing, terrain, etc.—may not be ideal for you.

• There may be other people involved who are willing to help your opponent defeat you.

• Since time and endurance may not be on your side, you must strike the first and final blow in order to end the fight quickly.

But since life seems to imitate art, a number of people who haven't been initiated into the art of street brawling still think fights start and end like the ones on the screen. While these cinematic encounters may look real (and they certainly seem exciting), actual street confrontations aren't so pretty. I've heard several stories firsthand about normal folks who were attacked while walking down the street and killed with a single punch to the head. Not injured, not knocked unconscious, but killed, as in dead and not moving!

Since I'm obviously interested in the subject, I immediately asked a number of questions about the attacks: Did the assailants use a weapon? No, just their fists. Did the attackers hit the victims more than once? No, just one shot to the side of the head, near the temple. Did the attackers "ambush" their victims? Yes, as far as we can determine. Did the victims strike their heads on anything else as they fell? Possibly, although it's not clear if striking the ground added more to an already fatal injury.

KEY: These stories make two points absolutely clear: When you're out on the streets, you need to have "eyes in the back of your head" at all times, and, more importantly, you *can* be mortally wounded by a single punch to the head. The ruthless animals who murdered their victims know these facts, don't they? You should too.

FIST BLOWS

What we've learned about fighting in the movies and on TV has told us that a punch to the face offers a tried-and-true method for putting an opponent on the ground. Boxing matches offer the same conclusion: a hard shot to the head will put a man on the canvas. While this much is apparent from just looking at the end results of TV programs, movies, or boxing fights, what really matters is not so much the ability to strike the opponent's head but to do it with power and accuracy.

If you have both power and accuracy in your strikes, you'll win your fight. If you have one and not the other but you have some luck on your side, you'll probably come out on top as well. You may be able to put someone on the deck with a powerful shot that isn't particularly accurate—a hard punch to the area just below the ear, for example—or you may be able to get in an accurate blow to the jaw that doesn't have much "oomph" behind it but still serves your purpose. However, if you have neither power nor accuracy (nor luck), you'll probably take a hit yourself and lose the encounter.

Just like a professional baseball player knows everything about the tools of his trade—his gloves and his bats—so should you know about the fighting tools at your disposal, starting with your fists.

Punching something correctly—a jaw, a rib cage, a kidney—is not as easy as it looks. You have to know how to get ready to hit and then how to hit, so the following primer on basic fisticuffs is in order:

• Learn to "curl" your fists before you strike. Start by folding your fingers and placing the fingertips up at the very top of your palm. Now curl your fingers into a fist, dragging the tips across your palm as you do. Grip the thin fold of skin inside your fist tightly. Curling your fist inside itself like this can really add to your punching power. It also helps to protect your hand from injury by providing an internal cushion of skin.

• Lay your thumb out of the way, near the second and third knuckles. Don't put it inside the fingers of your fist or have it stick out in any fashion, unless of course you enjoy breaking this delicate appendage when you strike something.

• Keep your wrist straight and locked at all times—not pointing up or down. Form a solid, hard line from your wrist across to your forearm. Not only is this "straight line" more powerful, it acts as a shock absorber to prevent nasty bone breaks in the wrist. You'll notice that in the weight-lifting gym, most good bench pressers use this straight strong-wrist

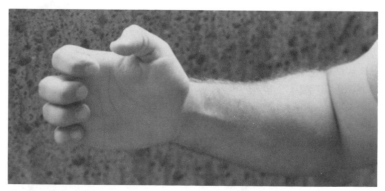

START "CURLING" YOUR FIST . . .

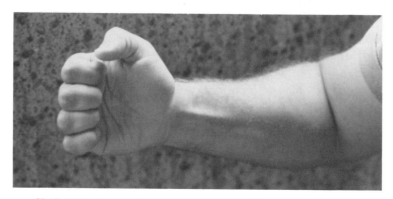

. . . GRAB YOUR PALM PADS WITH YOUR FINGERTIPS . . .

. . . AND ROLL YOUR HAND INTO A TIGHT FIST.

NEVER HIT ANYTHING WITH A FIST AND WRIST LIKE THIS!

technique as a better way to distribute the weight of the heavy bar across their wrists and arms.

• Aim to hit your target area with the first two knuckles on your hand. These are the strongest in your knuckle repertoire. Hitting a glancing blow with your last two knuckles could break these delicate bones.

• As you strike, focus on your target area primarily and your opponent's entire body secondarily. This sounds harder than it is. Use your peripheral vision to keep his entire form in view and focus most of your attention on the B.E.A.T. model area you want to attack. Aim for a finishing point at least 3 feet past your attacker's body. This technique of "punching past" your target will add more power to your movements.

Fist Position Basics

Anytime you use your fists in an offensive manner, you have several position choices: front fist blows, side fist blows, backfist blows, uppercut blows, half fist blows, knuckle point blows, and, finally, "hammer fist" blows.

Which of these seven you choose to use depends upon the situation, the size and strength of your attacker, and how close or far way you are from him and his target zones. Some work extremely well in certain instances and not so good in others. Some depend upon your own strength levels and others rely on accuracy instead of brute power. As with anything you read in this book, take what works best for you and improve upon it. Keeping the B.E.A.T. model in mind—Brains, Eyes, Abdomen, Testicles—review the following fist attacks.

Front Fist Applications

This is the standard "knock out" punch position. Here, your palms face downward and you punch straight into your target. This is a highly effective blow, provided you use the proper hand technique—curl your fist, straighten your wrist, hit with the first two knuckles, etc.—and strike the proper target zones.

Keep this punch away from bony foreheads, cheekbones, and skulls. Using the B.E.A.T. model as your reference point and going from the enemy's top to bottom, aim your front fist punches to the sides of his jaw, his nose, his temple, the area below his ear, and, lastly, his eye sockets.

Moving downward, step into the opponent and strike the abdomen, solar plexus,

A HARD SHOT TO THE BELLY WILL PUT HIM DOWN.

IF YOU CAN GO LOW, GO LOW AND HIT HIM
WHERE HE LIVES.

and especially the vulnerable "short rib" cage area underneath his armpits.

KEY: Focus your abdominal front fist punches into the soft area surrounding the navel and remember to punch through and past your target as if you wanted to lift your opponent off his feet.

Since there are no rules in streetfighting situations (save for two: win and leave), nothing says you can't use a front fist punch to your opponent's testicles. If you aren't one of those rare people capable of doing a split, just drop to one knee as your assailant rushes in and apply the front fist punch with all your might. In some rare cases where your attacker is quite a bit taller than you, you may not need to do anything other than bend slightly to reach this vulnerable zone.

Side Fist Applications

The side fist punch is thrown like the front fist save for the position of your hand. With the front fist, your palm faces down as you punch. During the side fist punch, your hand rotates upward so that your thumb points up and your palm is now "bladed" in a sideways position. While the front fist punch usually springs from shoulder height, the side fist typically gets unleashed from waist level. Coming from this height and position offers you the opportunity to generate tremendous power using hip torque.

While you can certainly use the side fist punch to attack targets at the head and face, it's a much more effective weapon when aimed at the abdomen, ribs, kidneys, and testicles. The side fist punch also works best when you are standing in a bladed or sideways position near your opponent. From this protected position, you can "shoot" the side fist out from your own waist level and attack his ribs, solar plexus, and kidneys.

Remember to keep good fist position techniques in mind as you execute this movement. The fist protectors you learned for the front fist blow apply here too.

KEY: The side fist punch is not a sweeping movement. It does not curl around your body as it heads to the attacker. It is a snapping, straight-on shot that comes from waist level. It does not loop or swing around to get to the target. It shoots out and back in one quick motion.

Backfist Applications

The back knuckle strike can be a real life-saving movement. Done correctly, this highly devious attack can come from nowhere to jar your opponent out of his senses and ultimately out of the battle. Unlike front or side fist punches that have

THE SIDE FIST PUNCH SHOOTS STRAIGHT OUT FROM THE HIP. AIM FOR MIDDLE AND LOW TARGETS WITH IT.

a tendency to telegraph themselves, the back knuckle seems to fly into your attacker's face as if by magic. Better still, the fist shape and design of the back knuckle can do tremendous damage to your opponent's target zones.

Learning to hit effectively with the backfist first requires you to review the principles of good punching technique. Everything is the same, except for the wrist position. With the front and side fist blows, your wrist should be rock-solid straight in order to protect your hand and forearm bones from injury. The back knuckle is similar in every respect except this time your wrist is slightly bowed in an outward direction. This bowing-out adjustment helps you to put your first two knuckles on to the target zone.

To be most effective, this punching movement requires speed, power, and accuracy. Above all, you must hit your target directly, as this punch can leave you wide open to a brutal counterattack. Anytime you initiate a backfist strike, keep the following things in mind:

THIS BACKFIST PUNCH WILL HIT HIS NOSE AND EYE SOCKET SIMULTANEOUSLY.

• Strike with the top two knuckles only! Never hit anything with the back of your hand. There are highly sensitive nerves and small, tender bones in the back of your hand that will swell and ache to no end should you miss-hit with them. Stay on target and hit with the knuckles first and only!

• Use the back knuckle wisely. Hit to the target zones that were made for the movement. Drive your knuckles into the attacker's temple, jaw side, ear hole, eye socket, and side of the nose. Stay away from any B.E.A.T. target below the neck. There usually isn't enough power in the backfist to do any real damage at lower heights.

• Once you've struck the target with the back knuckle, don't let your arm and fist just hang there. Like any other punch, the backfist is a snapping, "hit and return" movement. Throw the backfist, hit the target, and whip your hand back to the original position near your body. Letting your hand fall straight down in front of you will risk a counterattack or a grab by your opponent.

• Think of your first two knuckles as if they were a small battering ram. Use the backfist move to drive and dig those knuckles into your opponent's head and face target zones. Hit as hard as you can and be prepared to follow this movement up with a front or side fist should the fight continue.

• As with all of your other punches, get proficient from both sides of your body. Since most people are right-handed, they tend to "square off" in a strong side right-handed fighting pose—right foot and right fist back, left foot and left fist forward. Practice at home, in the gym, or in front of a full-length mirror until the back knuckle movement feels smooth from both your strong and weak hand side.

This book doesn't spend much time teaching you fancy spinning techniques like you see in every Chuck Norris movie. These airborne spinning kicks and occasional spinning punches look great on film, but in reality they require tremendous practice and good coordination to perfect. If you're really interested in learning spinning rear, crescent, or heel hook-type kicks, enroll in a qualified martial arts studio and get some good instruction.

However, my favorite spinning movement of all time fits in nicely with the backfist strike. Best yet, it's much easier to learn than a spinning kick and it can generate enough force to do twice as much damage as a standard back knuckle move.

If you mix a spinning movement with a back knuckle movement, you get a "spinning back knuckle." This move is a great fight ender and can induce mountains of pain in your attacker. It relies on speed, target acquisition, and surprise to deliver a heavy knockout blow to your opponent's face.

From a bladed, sideways stance, face your attacker with your left foot forward and your hands cupped loosely at your waist. In one continuous motion, drop your rear (right or strong) hand to your side and turn in a clockwise direction, putting your back to your opponent ever so briefly. As he stands there wondering what you plan to do, continue to turn clockwise and cock your right fist into a bowed-out back knuckle. As you come around to face him again, launch your right backfist into his temple, eye socket, nose, or other suitable target. When you've finished the movement, you should be in the opposite stance as when you began—with your right (or strong side) forward.

Slowly practice this spinning backfist in front of a large mirror until you have the footwork and the position change down correctly. Remember to keep both of your hands up as you execute the movement. One hand will strike your opponent and the other will protect your face from any incoming blows.

KEY: In an actual situation, this technique is not for the slow-footed. Speed and the element of surprise make it effective. Work on the speed here.

Uppercut Applications

The uppercut blow is a close-quarters movement. If you can smell your attacker's body odor or bad breath, you're probably close enough to use this attack effectively. Don't try to use an uppercut punch to the jaw or the ribs unless you can reach your attacker with ease. If you miss with this punch, it can take many precious seconds to get back into position and launch another assault.

However, if you do find yourself close enough to your enemy to use the uppercut, it has a great reputation as a fight-ender. A solid shot to the fleshy underside of the jaw, a tongue-biting punch thrust up to the chin, or a hard punch to the abdomen that starts at your toes and ends

THE SPINNING BACK FIST TAKES SKILL, BUT IT CAN COME OUT OF NOWHERE TO BLAST YOUR OPPONENT.

AS YOU TURN YOUR BODY, YOUR HEAD SHOULD ALREADY BE LOOKING AT THE TARGET.

at the top of your enemy's forehead can take the wind out of even the most determined fighter's sails.

The uppercut is a difficult punch to master, but in the right circumstances it can chip teeth, break jaws, or snap rib bones. The secret of success with the

punch lies not so much in your hands, but rather, in your hips. Unless you're especially strong, the uppercut is not too effective as a flat-footed punch. You must gather your momentum from below your hips and abdomen and drive upward in a short, tight arc off your toes.

The best way to practice the uppercut

WHIP YOUR BACKFIST PUNCH PAST YOUR TARGET FOR EVEN MORE TORQUE AND POWER.

is to imagine that your elbows are glued to your hip bones. Plant the points of your elbows deep into your hip bones and—from this slightly stooped position—launch your punches upward, using hip torque and the strength of your calves to get up on your toes.

THE UPPERCUT SHOULD SPRING FROM YOUR HIP TO HIS JAW.

A full-length mirror and access to a boxing heavy bag will help you with the footwork and hand positions. Remember that for an uppercut to cause more damage to your opponent than you, you'll have to use good fist position—palms facing you, wrists straight up and not bent, and first two knuckles into the target.

Half Fist Applications

The half fist punch may not sound too threatening, and you certainly won't scare yourself by making one. But it does have a very specific application that makes it quite effective for streetfighting. Whereas the front, side, and uppercut blows have a number of useful targets to choose from, the half fist goes after one vital spot—the throat.

To make the half fist, make a front fist, keep the wrist straight, and make sure your palm is facing the floor. Now open your hand and point the fingers out from your palm. Then curl just your fingers back to the pads of your upper palm, being careful not to bend your hand at the knuckles. In effect, you've created half of a fist, hence the name. Make sure you tuck your thumb in so it doesn't get caught on anything.

To throw the half fist, you'll need to be in close to your op-

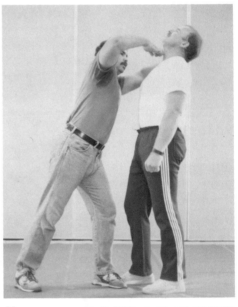

USE HIS HAIR OR CLOTHING AS AN ANCHOR AND HIT HIS THROAT WITH YOUR MIDDLE KNUCKLES. LIKE ALL THROAT SHOTS, THIS IS A DANGEROUS TECHNIQUE.

ponent. It works particularly well when you have hold of some portion of his body or clothing, especially his shirt or hair. If you can reach around and grab the back of his hair (ponytails make the easiest targets) or his shirt or jacket and pull his head back to expose his throat, you can shoot a quick half fist right into this vulnerable spot.

KEY: *This is a dangerous punch with life-ending potential.* A hard blow to the windpipe can merely stun your enemy enough for you to get out of the situation, or it just may crush his larynx and windpipe, thereby ending his fighting days altogether. *Use this movement only as a last-ditch effort to save your life.*

Good hand position, speed, and accuracy are the secrets to an effective half fist. It's a great close-in blow with the capacity to do significant damage. If you're trapped by the opponent's body, grab his clothes or hair, throw a half fist into his throat, and then let him hit the deck.

Knuckle Point Applications

Like the half fist, the knuckle point blow has its own limited applications. While it's not a fight stopper, the knuckle point or "eagle beak" punch can incapacitate your assailant long enough to give you time to prepare another harder attack.

To make the eagle beak, make a side fist first, with the wrist straight and the palm bladed to the ground. Extend only your middle finger knuckle and use your thumb to anchor this position down tight. With this second knuckle protruding out, your fist almost looks like the business end of a shovel. And that's exactly what the knuckle point punch will do for you—"dig" into your opponent.

The targets for this spearing side fist punch include the armpits and short ribs, the eye sockets, and in a unique application, the tops of your attacker's hands. In this last area, you can create a significant dysfunction if you rap the top of your assailant's hand in between and just below his first and second fingers. A nerve of some size runs through here, and a hard, well-placed blow can shut down his whole hand. Keep this rare spot in mind if you are grabbed and have time to respond. (Refer back to my discussion of the striking position of the back knuckle for reasons

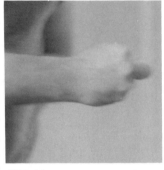

THE KNUCKLE POINT ACTS LIKE A SHOVEL TO DIG INTO

why you don't want to land a backfist strike with anything other than your first two knuckles.)

The eagle beak punch is a quick, back-and-forth blow that serves to strike the opponent where he is vulnerable. Using the B.E.A.T. model as a guide, you can use it to hit the eyes, ear holes, sides of the neck, and front of the throat. It's also quite effective around the upper rib cage, but try to avoid the fleshy parts of the abdomen since the punch won't do much damage there.

Finally, the testicles make a good target since the eagle beak punch is such a bony striking movement. You may want to drop to one knee and snap the knuckle point punch into this target.

Hammer Fist Applications

Recall how I mentioned earlier that you will need to learn to use your fighting tools before you can successfully engage in a street confrontation. The hammer fist can become the best "tool" in your box.

In terms of the B.E.A.T. model, the hammer fist is a specific lower-target blow. It works best when aimed at the testicles. The name is not a misnomer, either. The hammer fist blow looks and feels just like hammer—snapping out and going back in a big, damaging hurry.

To make the hammer fist, start by curling your fist as with

all of the other punching movements, only make sure it's really a tight seal. The best hammer fist strikes are the ones made by the "hardest" hands. Unlike the other fist moves using the first two knuckles, the half fist knuckles, or the "eagle beak" knuckle, the hammer fist uses the bottom edge of the fist as its striking point.

To use this side of your fist correctly, you must be in the proper position. In essence, the hammer fist is made from a crouching position, sort of a bend-at-the knees stance. Moreover, the hammer fist works best if you turn your back slightly on your opponent. This rear-facing position helps in three ways: it gets you into a low stance that gives you better access to the target (testicles), it protects the rest of your body from harm as you initiate the move, and it puts you in a position to make your immediate escape after throwing the punch.

To set up for the hammer fist, bend your knees slightly and pivot on your toes so that you almost turn your back to

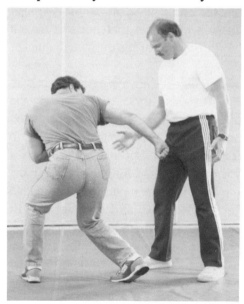

your enemy. Bend your elbow up high near your body and cock your fist to make the strike. When the assailant gets close enough, unleash the hammer fist to the target and pound him with the curled and bottom part of your fist. This movement is second only to a swift front snap kick to the balls and will drop even the bravest of souls.

YOU'LL HAVE TO CROUCH SLIGHTLY TO GET THE HAMMER FIST ON TARGET.

As with every other punch in your

arsenal, don't let the hammer fist linger near your opponent's body. Get your arm and body into position and let it fly, but then bring it back home just as quickly as you shot it out.

Other Effective Fist Blows

Saving your butt in a streetfight requires you to get the immediate upper hand, finish the problem, and then get the hell out. The best way to get the jump on your enemy is to do something completely outrageous, surprising, or even daring. Come at him in a way he would never possibly expect. Make noise, act like a crazy person, scream obscenities, and generally look abnormal, dangerous, and very aggressive in those critical split seconds before you launch your attack.

I've seen one wily fighter pretend to take off his wrist watch and use a whipping back knuckle move to smash the glass crystal into his opponent's shocked face. I've heard about other people who drop their wallet on the ground and then kick the mugger in the teeth when he stupidly bends down to pick it up. I know a man who pretended to have a seizure and then beat the stuffing out of his outwitted attacker when he came too close.

Time and motion studies tell us it's always easier to act than to react. This means he who fights first usually wins. By the time the attacker's punch is fired at your head, it's probably too late for you to move out of harm's way. You may be able to parry the blow or block it somewhat, but in most cases, if it catches you off-guard you could spend a long afternoon in the dentist's chair having your front incisors replaced.

One of the best ways to surprise and dismantle your opponent is to punch him in an area where he's never been hit before, like the side of the neck, the abdomen, or the testicles. Don't always swing for the face. You could risk injury to your hand bones, and you may miss if he ducks. Go lower first—abdominal and testicle blows are always a good surprise.

For an ever greater surprise, try another favorite technique of mine: the double fist blow. In this powerful fight ender, you

THIS DOUBLE PUNCH IS EASY TO DO AND HARD TO STOP.

double-punch your assailant with one high blow to the nose and one low blow to the testicles. The movement is easy and natural after a little practice, and the results are guaranteed to please you and devastate him.

Put your top fist into a front fist position—knuckles ahead, palm facing down—and put your bottom fist into an uppercut position— knuckles ahead and palm facing up. Position the two fists in front of you about even with your own nose and groin and step forward and fire away, punching straight at each target zone simultaneously.

Practice this technique in front of a large mirror, on a gym heavy bag, or with a partner until you get the angles, fist positions, and forward-moving footwork down right. This move hits your attacker in two B.E.A.T. model areas at once. He may be able to block one of the incoming blows, but I'll bet the other one catches him completely off-guard and puts him down.

KEY: Like the spinning backfist, speed and the element of surprise are vital here. If your opponent eludes the attack, your entire middle is exposed.

CHAPTER 3

Chops, Palm Strikes, Ridge Hands, and Finger Tears

"Keep violence in the mind where it belongs."

—Nelson Algren

The last chapter ended with a unique two-fisted double-punching movement that is sure to catch your opponent by surprise. It's a novel way to attack two vital spots at once, and it should illustrate that there are an infinite number of ways to disable a street hood bent on harming you.

Further, your own personal streetfighting approach should be flexible enough to allow you to use whatever weapons are at the ready. In the previous chapter, I discussed the best fist movements and explained when and how to apply them. In this chapter and the one that follows, I'll suggest other hand attack techniques that bring entirely different strikes into play. You'll learn of new ways to use your hands to stop an attacker.

Flexibility, in this sense, is the ability to choose and use whatever will get the job done. Fist work, as you will see, is not the only way to bring down the mighty.

KEY: Whether you're practicing alone at home or in a gym

or martial arts studio with a partner, keep your target zones in mind. Use your own eye level and body position to "air strike" your B.E.A.T. model targets when you practice. Burn those areas into your memory banks. In a stressful street problem situation, you will revert back to how you have trained. Assaults can happen in poor lighting conditions, in unfamiliar locales, in bad weather, on broken ground, and even on the side of a freeway. You should be able to react to any real provocation just like you've trained yourself to.

Fighting with your hands requires some quick preparation before you attack. You must learn to get your body ready before you can punch. Make sure your head is pointing toward your target; get your shoulders "squared" to be able to twist forward as you punch; get in a bladed stance with your strong-side leg back and your weak-side leg forward; get one hand up to protect your head when you punch; and make sure your hips are turned toward the target and your feet are planted and ready to unleash all of your body's torquing power.

While this may sound just like preparing to hit a golf ball—"knees bent, hands relaxed, shoulders over the ball," etc.—your mind and body are smart enough to place themselves in the ready position if you've given them the proper training.

CHOPPING BLOWS

In some situations, using fists may not be your best choice. Hand chops, because of their unique shape and whipping motion, can help you attack certain exposed areas better than fist blows.

Anytime an attacker grabs you from the front, he is putting himself at risk of receiving a nasty chop to the top of his forearm. Several large motor nerves run through the top of the forearm muscles, and a hard, hand-edge chop to this region can create dysfunction in your opponent.

Further, chopping movements can get you closer to your opponent—his "inside" position—where you can attack two vital spots—the throat and the testicles.

Throat Chops

Since the dawn of man, the throat has been a target for humans interested in killing one another. Prehistoric man spent much of his time watching animals. He quickly learned that animals dispatched their foes by biting and tearing out the sensitive throat. He took this knowledge back to his own wars and battles, striking and cutting at the throats of his enemies as a way to kill them.

As I stated in my discussion of half fist throat shots in the previous chapter, you have to recognize this area as a potentially fatal danger zone. With that in mind, know too that for a throat chop to work effectively, you must be able to hit the target squarely. Glancing chop blows off your opponent's bony head, shoulder muscles, or jaw bone probably won't do much to stop him.

For a throat chop to really incapacitate him, you'll have to be able to "snake" your hand into the space between his chin and chest or into the side area between his shoulder and the side of his head. This is not always as difficult as it sounds. In some fighting situations, your adversary will expose his neck and throat during his attacking movements or as a result of your first punch.

Remember that the neck chop and the throat chop have highly specific uses, different than their punch counterparts. The neck chop serves to stun your attacker and water his eyes with pain. If it lands on the proper nerve zone, it also can cause a momentary loss of muscle coordination. Your attacker may be unable to lift his arm on the chopped side or turn his head in that direction, at least temporarily. This can give you a few valuable seconds to finish the encounter or make your escape.

The throat chop has one specific purpose: stop your opponent's attack immediately. The intense pain and the sudden shortness of breath that follow a throat chop blow can give you the edge in any street battle.

Like fist blows, chopping blows should "shoot" out and back. Don't let them linger near your opponent; fire them into the neck or throat crevice and then snap them back. And like certain fist blows that require you to be close to your attacker—half fists, hammer fists, etc.—most chopping movements are useless unless you are close enough to hit what you aim for.

A NECK CHOP USES THE HARD EDGE OF YOUR HAND TO HURT NERVES, MUSCLES, AND ARTERIES.

KEY: From my experience, I've noticed that the martial artists with the hardest chops are also well-built, well-muscled folks. Strong forearms and powerful biceps, triceps, and shoulders will add more "snap" to your chops.

A well-placed chop to the side of your enemy's neck can stun him momentarily enough for you to get in position to use a fist blow or a kick. A hard front chop to his exposed throat can also cause him to lose all interest in attacking you and spend his next moments gasping for air. Even the slightest knock to the delicate throat will cause internal and external bruising sufficient enough to make normal breathing difficult. A powerful throat chop—like a hard half fist blow—can

cause significant damage to your assailant's soft internal tissues.

Testicle Chops

To chop your attacker's testicle area, just duplicate the hammer fist position, but change the hand position from a strong hammer fist to a strong hand chop. Use the hard, bladed outer edge of your hand to make the strike. The foot position, the slight crouch, and the quick in-and-out

NOTE THE HAND AND BODY POSITION ON THE TESTICLE CHOP. IT'S SIMILAR TO AN OPEN-HANDED HAMMER FIST.

movement are exactly the same as your hammer fist attack.

Accuracy, snapping force, quick hand speed, and the ability to follow through with other hand, fist, or feet blows in combination are the keys to effective chop movements.

PALM STRIKE BLOWS

Whenever you lock your car door and it fails to close all the way, you're faced with a decision: "Do I try to close it with my hip and risk denting the door, or do I hit it with my palm and risk hurting my hand?"

Choose your palm, and not just because you'll do less damage to your car. Just remember to pull your fingers back far enough out of the way and use the "butt" of your palm to tap the errant door. A healthy palm strike will close it and give you some free practice for the streets.

Seriously, palm strikes offer another unique way to incapacitate your assailant. Even though the palm is a small tool, you can generate tremendous force with it. A hard palm strike to any number of upper and lower B.E.A.T. model targets can work just as well as a hard punch.

A PALM STRIKE TO THE CHIN WILL HELP HIM BITE HIS TONGUE AND CHIP SOME TEETH.

There are three secrets to a powerful palm strike: good hand position, good momentum, and a good target choice. Put them all together and you have another arrow for your quiver, another bullet for your magazine, and another grenade to hang on your streetfighting belt.

Hand position is critical because any deviation in your approach could cause you to catch your hand on something other than what you aimed for. Missing your target or jamming your fingers is a good way to quickly break a bone. Whether you choose an upper palm strike (fingers and thumb curled back and pointing up in the air) or the lower palm strike (fingers and thumb curled and pointing down to the ground), make sure you strike only with the area at the base of your wrist joint. This area—where your "lifeline" hand crease ends—is hard and sturdy enough to cause damage to your opponent's B.E.A.T. model targets: his nose, ear hole, under his chin, abdomen, and testicles.

The nose is a great upper-zone target because you can catch

THIS UNIQUE DOUBLE PALM STRIKE TO THE LOWER ABDOMEN WILL HIT THE INTESTINES AND BLADDER.

him in the ridge below his nose and above his upper lip. This area is rich with blood vessels and covers a major nerve. Any pressure on this nerve can cause blinding pain. Test for yourself by using the side of your index finger to push in and up above your upper lip and toward your nose.

Striking your attacker's chin with an upward palm strike can cause him to bite his tongue, chip his teeth, and even lose consciousness as his jaw joints collide with each other.

You can generate sufficient force for your upper or lower palm strikes by winding up like a windmill. Swing your arms forward and pop your palms into his face or swing your arms backward and double-strike your palms into his abdomen in two places. Or try simultaneously palming his ears or crushing his kidneys from behind.

The best lower palm strike target is, of course, the testicles. You can pop this area with a quick palm strike, making sure your fingers are curled back and your elbows lock into position at the end of the striking movement.

Hand position is important as always. When you palm-strike upper targets, point your fingers up and your palm down. When you palm-strike lower targets, point your fingers down and your palm up. Instincts and practice will help you make the right positioning choices when the time comes.

RIDGE HAND BLOWS

Like the chopping movements, ridge hand blows will help to stun your opponent and give you time to get into position to finish the problem. The ridge hand gets its name from the striking area—literally, the ridge or top of your inner hand, along the line formed by your index finger and thumb web. This bony protrusion will fit perfectly into your opponent's temple, side of his neck and throat, and testicles.

As with the half fist, the neck and throat chops, and the palm strikes, keep your thumb tucked away when you shoot the ridge hand out and back. Leaving your thumb out in the breeze only asks for it to be broken.

Unlike most of the other hand blows in this book, the upper ridge hand is fired in an arcing motion. It comes from around your waist, up toward your own head level, and angles down to the temple or neck target.

Conversely, the lower ridge hand shoots out and back from your own groin level as it strikes your opponent. Keep your weak hand up by your face to ward off any counterattack and jam that hard hand bone into the testicle target zone.

The ridge hand is also particularly useful as a defensive attack. If your assailant lunges towards you and his head drops below the height of your head, feel free to step to the side and whack the ridge hand against his temple or neck. Similarly, you can thrust a lower ridge hand to the testicles as you back away from your enemy. And if he tries to back away from you, follow his path and shoot the ridge hand to his balls as he tries to move out of your way.

TEARING MOVEMENTS

Human flesh tears rather easily. Unlike alligators and rhinos, we have soft skin. You can soak your face in saltwater like boxing great Jack Dempsey used to do, or you can pound your knuckles against an iron plate like the Chinese kung fu masters, but there really isn't much you can do to toughen up your fleshy hide.

Tearing movements can cause significant damage to your opponent if you ever get the opportunity to use them. Unfortunately, only a few of us ever walk around naked in the streets, so you'll have to choose your applications of flesh-ripping techniques wisely.

The best targets for flesh tears—or "avulsions" as they are called by the medical community—are those that are potentially weak by virtue anyway. If we trace the B.E.A.T. model from head to toe, we see a number of worthy and tearable regions:

• *Eye sockets.* No secret here. Dig your fingers into the eye socket and pull away, just as if you were starting a lawn mower engine by yanking hard on the cord. Pull your finger toward the outside of his eye socket—in the direction of his ear—and "flick" your fingernail through this delicate tissue. One of these attacks and the fight is over for him. Finish up with fists or vote with your feet and leave.

USE YOUR FINGERTIPS TO DIG AND TEAR THE EYELIDS.

• *Eyelids.* Same thing, different place. If you can "pick" at his eyelids as if you were lifting a nickel off the ground, you will do heavy damage. If you're successful with this ultimate tearing movement, let's hope your attacker can get to a good eye surgeon in time.

• *Ears.* As grisly as this sounds, this *is* a streetfight we're talking about. Grab the ear and pull hard down to the ground. Unless he wants to leave his hearing appendage in your hand, he will go down and go down hard. Feel free to encourage this gravity and pain-based movement by shoving him with your other hand or providing a hard fist blow or kick as he falls. The tissue that attaches the ear to the head is thin and sinewy. Pull as though you were trying to pick a ripe orange off a tree.

GRAB THE EAR AND GIVE IT A HEALTHY TUG DOWNWARD.

• *Mouth.* As unhygienic and dangerous as this sounds, you'd be surprised at how often the opportunity arises for you to stick a hooked finger into your amazed enemy's mouth and pull his cheek skin off the frame. This odd move gets a hearty "as a last resort only" qualification, but the impact on your attacker is unforgettable.

• *Neck skin, inner biceps skin, hair pull.* Each of these has its applications and uses. The fleshy area around your assailant's neck offers a unique sort of dual handhold for you to grab and twist. I have heard about one fight where the attacker grabbed both sides of his opponent's neck flesh and twisted and pulled with all his might. As the other party tried

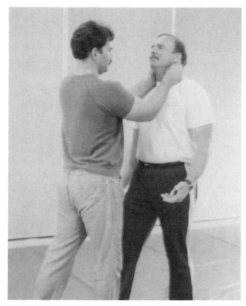

GRAB THIS SENSITIVE NECK SKIN AND PULL DOWN OR OUT. THIS WILL BRING TEARS TO HIS EYES.

to get out of this painful hold, the attacker headbutted him for all he was worth. The fight, as you can imagine, ended immediately.

For all of its size and strength, the skin around your inner biceps is thin and subject to heavy bruising. One of my kung fu san soo instructors grabbed me by the arm and twisted a small piece of my biceps flesh as he shoved my face down. I was concentrating so hard on the shooting pains in my arm that I almost forgot to put a hand out to prevent my face from smashing the mat.

When I was in grade school, hair pulling seemed to be the sport of choice for a number of little boys. The targets or the "pullees" didn't seem to matter—other little girls and other little boys with any amount of hair at all were at risk. Strangely, some people seem almost immune to a hearty hair pull while others scream if even one follicle gets yanked out. Use the hair pull to gain time and distance from your opponent, to cause immediate pain, or to get at another target like the throat or neck.

• *Testicle sack.* Another target for the "strange but true" files. While the testicles themselves make an appropriate target in almost every street confrontation, the actual sack itself is a quiet favorite among knowledgeable martial artists. If you're in close-quarters or grappling with your opponent, reach down and grab the testicle sack and give a sharp and immediate upward or downward pull. The fight, I assure you, will end in your favor.

KEY: Don't be afraid to put "hands-on" in the groin area. This is not an ice cream social; this is the streets, where someone or a whole group of his pals will want to put a hurtin' on you. If you can punch, chop, or grab at the groin to save your skin, do it.

THE TESTICLE SACK IS FRAGILE. IT TEARS LIKE PAPER.

CLAW HANDS

I recall a passage from Watergate participant G. Gordon Liddy's compelling book *Will*. After he was sentenced to federal prison in California, he met a man while working out in the prison exercise yard. This Asian gentleman had "the look" of a modern-day warrior. Liddy, no secret to modern warfare himself, thought he recognized the man's inner strength and capacity for tremendous violence. In conversation, the man told Liddy how, as a young boy, his father had trained him in the ancient martial arts and even went so far as to break his son's thumbs and bend them back to form claw hands of sorts. He learned to use his disfigured hands as the ultimate punching, tearing, and clawing weapons.

Besides the terrifyingly obvious child abuse realities of this

CLAWING HIS WHOLE FACE FROM TOP TO BOTTOM WILL HIT HIS EYES, NOSE, AND MOUTH.

story, it does point out how the human body and, more directly, the human hands can wreak devastation and murderous pain on an opponent.

If you think of each of your fingers as if it had a long, sharpened fish hook attached to the end, and if you imagine that your thumb comes with its own built-in razor blade, you can create the effect of "claw hands."

Although claw hands don't strike like fist blows, you shouldn't discount their use. In appropriate close-quarters situations, you can use two or all of your fingers to form a deadly clawlike weapon. By attacking your assailant's face, eyes, and throat with a raking, pulling, tearing motion, you can blind him and tear at his flesh to such a degree that even the most dedicated battler will have to stop and regroup.

Using one hand alone or both hands—one right after the other—you can claw and strike at one or both of his eyes, his ears, his open mouth, and his throat. For maximum effectiveness, try letting your fingernails grow out enough to improve the scratching process.

SPEAR AND WEB HANDS

Here are two minor hand-fighting positions that you may

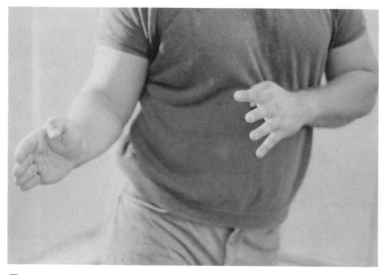

THE SPEAR HAND SHOOTS OUT AT WAIST LEVEL LIKE THE POINT OF A SWORD.

find useful in the right situations. With the spear hand, you attack your opponent's ribs and abdomen as if a small javelin were attached to your wrist. With the web hand, you try to drive the web area between your thumb and first finger into your attacker's throat.

I've seen people who can use their left and right spear hands so fast and so hard, it's not unlike being knifed by a sharpened bone. The key to this hand technique—as with all of the others—lies in the correct positioning of the fingers. You make the spear hand by curving your fingers slightly and bracing your thumb against the top of your hand. Keep your first and pinkie fingers straight and put a small arch into your middle and ring fingers. The spear hand movement is quick and sharp, almost as though you were trying to reach into your assailant's body and pluck out one of his ribs.

The web hand position is easy to create. Just pretend as though you wanted to reach inside your refrigerator for a cold can of beer. That C-curve position is a perfect replica of a good web hand. Fire the web hand up into your opponent's

THE WEB HAND LOOKS LIKE A C-CLAMP AND GRABS THE THROAT LIKE A VISE.

throat either as a windpipe striking movement or as a way to grab his throat to pull him down or push him back.

With either movement, keep your hands hard and tight. A limp-wristed spear or web hand could cause you to break a finger or thumb.

CHAPTER 4

Elbow and Knee Blows

"The wish to hurt, the momentary intoxication with pain, is the loophole through which the pervert climbs into the minds of ordinary men."
—Jacob Bronowski

The human elbow and the human knee serve as medical marvels. They are capable of generating tremendous physical force and yet they seem so maddeningly fragile. Watch any professional baseball or football team for a half season and several players will come down with elbow or knee ailments as a result of their activities on the field.

The elbow joint can crank out many pounds of pressure as it snaps your punches back and forth. Further, the ulna or lower arm bone that connects to the elbow joint is hard as nails. It makes—as this chapter will show you—a great striking tool. Although I've read no study to prove it, I'm convinced a fighter can hit much harder with his elbows than his fists, taking into account the short distance the elbow must travel to reach the target.

But for all of this strength and torque-wielding ability, the elbow is a tender joint. Any pro or even amateur baseball pitcher who can heave the ball at 80-90 miles per hour will almost always come down with some sort of elbow twinge at least once in his career. The tendons and cartilage rip and fracture easily, and they rest inside a joint that's bypassed by a few important nerves. Smashing one of these nerves between your elbow bone and a hard object can create intolerable pain as your not-so-funny bone aches and burns.

The knee joint is capable of handling several hundred pounds of load-bearing weight and can even operate in an up-and-down fashion with 1,000 lbs. strapped across the shoulders, as champion powerlifters have demonstrated during squat competitions. But even football players, track stars, and weight lifters—all with hugely muscled thighs—can be felled by even a slight tear to a single piece of cartilage that makes up the knee cap. Grown men who could run, block, and tackle anything moving on a field or lift and push prodigious amounts of weight in the gym are reduced to limping around with canes, crutches, and constant ice packs.

Like using your delicate hand bones, using your elbows and knees as streetfighting weapons is not without perils. The trick is knowing how and when to use these powerful tools and yet not cripple yourself in the process. Target acquisition with your elbow and knee strikes—which means hitting what you aim at—becomes crucial to your physical well-being. The only smashing of bones and crunching of tissues you'll want to hear (or feel) should come from your opponent's direction.

But enough warnings. In the right conditions, your elbows and knees can become a brutal set of battering rams, capable of putting your enemy down and out after the first application.

HITTING WITH THE ELBOW

The upper-target elbow strike is a personal favorite of mine. It's an in-your-face shot that can come out of nowhere to put your opponent down. And it also can lead into so many other movements and combinations of movements that it really serves as a stepping-stone move.

For best results, the elbow shot must be delivered from a position of proximity to your attacker. There's just no sense in trying to swing it in from left field. The best that will happen if you try to throw an elbow from too far is that you will miss. You may be able to recover and hit with it again, but in the worse case, your assailant will slaughter you with blows of his own.

This also can happen if you're too aggressive with your elbow swing. Missing your target will turn you sideways and give your opponent the chance to punch at your head and exposed ribs. If you use the elbow shot, be close and be on target.

From a purely physical standpoint, I like to think that the elbow shot is a "two-handed" movement. One "hand" (the elbow in this case) strikes at the target while the other hand either holds the target steady or, better yet, guides the target into the elbow strike itself. Fear not, for this is less confusing than it sounds, especially after you learn the elbow target zones.

Elbow Targets

The elbow strike is a sneaky weapon. You can fire it from a standing position while facing your opponent, from a standing position behind your opponent, or from a kneeling position facing or behind your opponent. How you throw it depends on your fighting situation, of course, but it surely adds flexibility, power, and impact to your fighting kit bag.

If you plan to hit with your right elbow, use your left hand to grab your opponent by the hair or clothing, preferably very near the area you want to strike. Anchor your hand on whatever you can grab and use it to pull your opponent's target (face, ribs, etc.) into the strike as it comes around.

KEY: When you use one hand to hold and the other to strike with the elbow, it's usually your "weak" or non-dominant hand that holds and your "strong" or dominant hand that strikes the target. Do whatever makes you feel comfortable, either by bringing your elbow to the target or bringing the target to your elbow.

Starting with your right fist close to your chest and your forearm parallel with the ground, sweep the hardened point of your right elbow into the target area in a right-to-left movement (or left-to-right if you use the left elbow). Let your momentum carry you into and past the target. If you can get the "push me/pull you" motion going for you by bringing the opponent into your elbow and your elbow into the opponent simultaneously, so much the better.

If you're facing your attacker and want to hit the upper areas, the primary and best target is his face—the bridge of and below his nose, under his chin, his teeth, temple, ear hole, neck, throat, or the side of his jaw.

A solid, side-moving, across-the-face elbow strike will work best if it's thrown hard and thrown fast. But remember that you don't always have to swing your elbow crossways when you hit; use an "upper-cut" elbow swing to help your assailant bite his tongue, chip a few teeth, and eat corn mush for the rest of his days. Just start with your tight-

AN ELBOW TO THE TEMPLE WILL KNOCK HIM OUT. NOTE THE POSITION OF THE NON-STRIKING HAND.

ened fist pointing up (palm facing toward you) and move your elbow upward in a hard, tight arc toward the point of his chin.

This uppercut elbow shot can be part of a terrific combination movement. After you've hit your assailant with an uppercut elbow and his head is snapped back, pop his nose with a back knuckle blow.

THE UPPERCUT ELBOW WILL LOOSEN HIS TEETH AND BREAK HIS JAW.

You're already in the neighborhood of his face anyway, and you can use the natural downward movement of your arm to reposition yourself correctly for a hard backfist to his face.

Practice both the crossing elbow and the uppercut elbow movements using your own face as a height guide. Let your elbow make a

YOU CAN USE THE UPPERCUT ELBOW FOR LOWER TARGETS, TOO.

satisfying smack into your opposite palm to gauge your striking power.

Don't stop after the first strike. Recock your elbow and fire it out again. Use an uppercut elbow blow, then a backfist, and follow them both with a crossing elbow shot. I've seen fighters grab their attackers in a tight grip and throw elbow shots into their faces 10 or 15 times in what seems like a split-second. Hard, repetitive elbow blows to your attacker's head will certainly stun him and may even knock him out. Don't bother to catch him as he goes down. Let the nice soft concrete pavement give you some extra hitting assistance.

KEY: By attacking the jaw, nose, and face, you can cause significant damage to your enemy without injuring yourself in the process. Remember that it's much easier to break the delicate mass of bones in your hand than the hard one in your elbow. This isn't to say that you can fire it out there risk-free, only that you have much less potential for injury if you use the elbow strike properly and with good form.

It is also possible to catch your attacker in his throat with a well-directed elbow. As with all other throat blows described in this book, consider the potential for life-

HITTING THE THROAT WITH AN ELBOW WILL CAUSE SEVERE INJURIES TO HIS BREATHING EQUIPMENT.

AIM FOR THE TEMPLE OR THE SIDE OF HIS FACE AS HE COMES INTO YOU.

threatening injury should you blast his tracheal region.

If his head is cocked back or you can reach his hair or clothing to get his neck exposed, follow it up with a crossing elbow shot, using the point of your elbow to dig into his throat. Think of this movement as a chopping blow, except you use your elbow instead of your hand.

The elbow strike is also a perfect finishing tool when you've delivered a fist blow or several combinations and your opponent is either moving or falling toward you in a downward spiral. As he goes past, use a downward elbow strike to "chop" the side of his head or neck and send him all the way to dreamland.

Moving to the middle level targets, you'll notice that the point of your elbow is perfect for driving across and through your opponent's abdominal region. His rib cage, solar plexus, and soft belly make excellent targets for your driving elbow. And since these regions are notoriously soft and easy to attack, you can do significant internal damage with a single elbow swipe.

But unlike with the face and head targets, you'll want to avoid multiple hits to these mid-range areas. Because the abdominal elbow strike is fired from a slight crouch position and because your opponent will have a tendency to fall on or across your body, don't linger in such close quarters. You could end up literally carrying your assailant for a few seconds as he collapses in pain toward you. Further, if your elbow blows are ineffective to his middle range—as may happen with unusually fat or well-muscled people—you could get punched hard for your troubles. Being close is not always the safest position. As with all strikes in this book, move in, hit,

NOTE HOW TO USE ALL OF YOUR BODY WEIGHT TO GIVE THE RIB SHOT MORE FORCE.

and move right out before he knows what to do or how to do it.

When we consider lower targets for the elbow strike, the old favorite—the testicles—springs to mind first. Just like the hammer fist blow to this zone, the elbow shot to the groin can work as a last resort to help you win the fight.

In most instances, to execute an elbow blow to the testicles, you'll need to be facing your opponent from a position quite near the ground. It works perfectly should you get knocked to the pavement and your attacker come in for what he thinks is the kill shot. Just imagine that your enemy's testicle area is shaped like his chin. With your fist tightened and your palm facing your chest, drive your elbow upward into this region and prepare to skittle out of the way as he tumbles toward you.

Besides the ever-popular testicles, the other good lower target zone is the knee joint. I read somewhere that it takes about 15 foot-pounds of hard pressure to crush this tender

joint. Should you find yourself in the vicinity of your assailant's locked and planted knee, execute an elbow strike across the inside or the outside of his kneecap, making sure to drive the point of your elbow all the way past his load-bearing joint. If it's done swiftly, even a glancing elbow blow to his

YOU CAN BUCKLE HIS KNEE JOINT WITH A HARD ELBOW SHOT.

locked knee will "unlock" it for him. A hard elbow strike to the knee can bring down any thug, even if he's built like a college linebacker.

For all the elbow strike targets you see when you face your opponent, there are an equal number of good ones from his rear. (For more information about how to

YOUR ELBOW IS MUCH HARDER THAN HIS NECK MUSCLES.

get behind your attacker in a street situation, review Chapter 1.)

From the top down, the soft area along the back of his neck makes an inviting target. Strike across this bone-and-tissue mass just like you would his face or jaw. A hard slam to this vital spot can send shock waves throughout his body, especially when he doesn't realize it's coming, since rear attacks often afford you the element of surprise.

Notice how your rib cage tends to wrap around your body and end along your back? This should point out that the elbow strike will do plenty of "short" or side rib damage from the rear, just as from the front.

The kidneys make another worthwhile elbow target. Make sure to hit across and in a downward direction to best reach them. If your attacker is wearing a heavy coat or bulky clothing, he probably won't feel your elbow shot to the kidneys or anywhere across the back for that matter. Choose your targets wisely, and be ready to make quick changes to match the situation.

Lastly, unlike few other strikes (save for the hammer fist to the testicles), the single or double elbow strike to the face or abdomen works well when *he* is behind you. Under these circumstances, your attacker has tried to grab you from behind. One or two quick elbow strikes to his face or stomach should back him

YOU CAN REALLY PUNISH HIS KIDNEYS WITH REPEATED ELBOW BLOWS.

away enough for you to get clear. Once you've stunned him and gained some distance, you can gather yourself and continue to press your own attack.

Practice single and double elbow strikes to the rear using your own body height as a guide. Lean slightly forward and concentrate on snapping your elbows into these high and low targets. They may not end the fight, but you can get enough time to break free of his grip and start with other fist movements.

KEY: The best way to train to use elbow strikes is with a heavy bag in the gym. Here you can get the feel for how hard to hit and how well your elbow bone and surrounding muscles take the shock. If you train in front of a full-length mirror, aim at the same height as your own nose, jaw, or abdomen. If you train "in the air" like this without the benefit of a bag, let your elbow strike smack into your guiding, open weak hand. This satisfying sound will help you gauge your intensity and energy for the blow as well as give you a little psychological boost.

BANGING WITH THE KNEE

While the elbow strike is a sneaky weapon, the knee strike is *really* a sneaky weapon. It can come from nowhere and quickly ruin your opponent's

DON'T BE AFRAID TO SWITCH SIDES AND HIT HIM WITH BOTH ELBOWS, ONE AFTER THE OTHER.

day. Whether it's aimed at his testicles or his face, it will do some damage to him.

The most important thing to remember about a knee strike is that you must generate force. Using the "bring it to your opponent" principle I discussed in the section on elbow strikes, try to create an intense driving movement that ends in a hard follow-through.

KEY: Just like with the elbow strike, try to bring the target down toward your knee as you bring your knee up toward the target. As his face or testicles come forward, your knee will already be on the way up to meet them and create a sufficient crunch.

Striking with the knee is not like kicking a football. You must keep your knee close and tucked toward your body, not out and away from it. As a test, stand on one leg and pull your knee into a cocked position. Place both hands on your knee and hold this whooping crane-like pose for a few seconds. This should show you how close your hands need to be to your kneecap to use this move correctly.

Targets for the knee strike include the abdomen, groin, and face. In each of these zones, try to grab your attacker and pull him down into quick contact

PULL HIM INTO YOUR KNEE AS YOU DRIVE INTO HIS ABDOMEN.

with your bent and upturned kneecap. If you can literally lift him off of his feet when you strike his abdomen, so much the better. If it feels as if you've driven his testicles up into his body cavity, you've used good form. And if you can create that "egg-cracking" face-into-knee sound that signifies the end of the fight, good for you.

Remember to keep your balance during all of the confusion and activity around you. To execute a knee strike, you'll have to stand on one leg, at least temporarily. This "flamingo" position can leave you vulnerable to be knocked down or to have your own planted knee injured by your assailant should he fall against it or kick at you.

To keep your balance, do the knee strike quickly! Any hesitation on your part can send you teetering to the pavement, possibly with your attacker on top of you. If you feel uncomfortable about your ability to stay on your feet, either practice the movement until you feel secure or practice standing on one foot for short periods of time, as all good martial artists can do.

Pull your knee up and hold it with both hands while you balance on one leg. Unless you have innate balance skills, you'll probably have some difficulty with this one. But in time, you'll be able to balance on one foot long enough to improve your knee strike "hang time."

THIS KNEE STRIKE WILL WORK BEST IF HE DIVES OR FALLS TOWARD YOU.

It should go without saying that the knee strike is an extremely close-quarters blow. Any attempt to hit some-one with your knee from too far away will not work. Get up close and personal with your assailant before you attempt it. Pull your enemy's face toward you and strike, holding the back of his head or clothing to get him to go lower. Grab his jacket near the lapels and drive upward with your knee into his abdomen or testicles.

THIS IS AN EXCELLENT BALANCE DRILL. AFTER YOU MASTER IT, TRY IT WITH YOUR EYES CLOSED.

With either elbow strikes or knee blows, most of your power will come from your hips. With elbow strikes, try to pivot and "torque" your hips into your target. With knee strikes, pivot and "thrust" your leg upward using good control and balance. Don't go get him with either striking movement. Bring his body to you and pound him.

CHAPTER 5

Foot Chops, Strikes, and Blows

"You should never have your best trousers on when you go out to fight for freedom and truth."
—Henrik Ibsen

Foot fighting—the use of your feet as striking weapons—brings with it the element of surprise. Most people fight forward and with their hands. Using your feet to kick and attack can intimidate and demoralize your enemy immediately. It makes him stop and think about what he has gotten himself into. Questions pop into his mind like, "What does this guy know that I don't? Is he a trained martial artist who will now proceed to kick my butt?"

You can do significant amounts of damage with your feet and all from a distance much farther than is necessary with your hands. You can cover more ground, strike in combinations, and still use your hands if needed. And all the while your opponent will not know what hit him. Street people expect you to fight with your hands. That's what they know and remember from television and the movies.

The only time you see someone fight with his feet on the screen is if it is an actual, labeled-as-such "martial arts movie." Otherwise, the bad guys and good guys duke it out with their fists. This incorrect "hands only" assumption alone will give you more than a large edge over your attacker if you choose to fight with your feet first.

One of the main reasons so few people fight with their feet is that it's not easy to do. Unless you have some formal martial arts training and a place to practice (a home gym, studio, etc.), you just can't develop the skills necessary to foot fight effectively.

Fighting with your feet means more than just kicking your attacker in the balls and stepping back (although that's not a bad strategy). Using your feet as weapons requires balance, focus, and the strength and ability to move the largest muscles in your body up, forward, and into a target that may already be on the move.

As effective as it looks and as devastating as it feels to your opponent, you will need to develop a certain amount of skill mixed with hard training to use it in the streets.

Just like there are a number of different ways to strike with your fists, there is a wide range of foot positions to use, depending on what you want to accomplish. Some positions work better than others because they are easy to learn and use. Other more complicated foot positions require more effort, but once you know them, you can strike with the extra confidence needed to win streetfights.

How well you fight with your feet ultimately depends on how your body is shaped. Long-legged, taller people with extended, tapered muscles in their legs seem to be better equipped to leg fight than short, stocky people with heavily muscled legs. If you have good genetics on your side—sturdy, whiplike legs, tough foot bones, and flexible hip joints—consider yourself lucky and ready to foot fight. If you weren't endowed with "perfect shaped" legs and feet, don't despair. Even if God didn't give you a fighter's body, you can still learn to strengthen and toughen your own tools for use in the street.

FRONT KICKS

Here's a breakdown of the different front foot positions and kicking techniques you'll want to learn and use. Practice them "in the air" to get comfortable with the timing and positioning before you move to a heavy bag. You can practice these movements in front of a full-length mirror and even work on them while lying on the floor and watching TV at home.

• *The front snap kick.* This is the granddaddy of all kicking movements. You face your opponent, split your legs slightly so that your "strong" or dominant leg is back, pull your knee up to waist level, and "snap" the kick into your attacker's abdomen, testicles, or, if you're really flexible, his chin.

Proper foot position for the front snap kick is important to the health and safety of the bones on the top of your foot. For

this kick, you can strike with a number of areas on your foot, including: the top, with the toes pointed down; the "ball," with the toes curled back toward you; and the heel, with your entire foot curled back.

In each example, a different and quite hard part of the foot strikes your opponent. The front snap kick with the toes pointed down is an excellent testicle smasher. The front snap "ball" kick

THE FRONT SNAP KICK USES THE TOP OF THE FOOT TO SMASH THE TARGET.

works well in the testicles, abdomen, and under the chin if you can reach it safely. And the front snap kick using the heel as the striking point can hammer your attacker in his abdomen, upper chest, and—with some skill—his chin.

The beauty of the front snap kick lies in its simplicity. It's not a very complex movement. By pulling your knee to waist level and firing the kick back and forth like a pump-piston, you can generate maximum force in minimum time. And just like a punch to the side of the jaw, the front snap kick is a perfect repeating kick. If one snap kick works good, maybe two or three will work even better. If your attacker fails to go down after the first kick, keep piling them on until he drops.

Your foot position is critical because you don't want to injure your toes. Even if they are covered by shoes, you can still break one or more toes. Practice the front snap kick with both legs until you can use the top, ball, and the heel of your foot with equal precision.

KEY: Train with your shoes on. It protects your feet and helps your balance. Don't train in your bare feet unless you never wear shoes in the street. Give your mind and body an edge by training in the same clothes you wear every day. If you wear construction boots, train with those. If you wear dress shoes, practice some kicks with those on your feet. Shoes also help bring extra damage to your body kicks and add power to your foot stomps to the knees, shins, and Achilles tendons. If your enemy is already knocked to the ground, feel free to stomp or kick his face and head.

• *The front snap scoop kick.* Everything is the same as with the regular front snap kick except this time you change not only your toe position but your follow-through and return as well. As you snap this kick, curl your toes back and aim for your assailant's testicles. As soon as you make contact with this target zone, lift up with your foot and pull back at the same time. This creates a "scooping" effect that drives in

and up into the target, hence the name.

The scoop kick is a specialized snap movement that relies on your ability to flex your toes upward and dig them into your attacker's testicles as you pull the kick back to the starting position. This movement works especially well when your enemy is wearing shorts. Practice it in front of a

NOTICE THE PULLED-BACK POSITION OF THE TOES ON THE FRONT SNAP SCOOP KICK.

mirror until you get the curled toe, hooking movement down.

• *The front push snap kick.* This is primarily a defensive weapon to get your attacker out of your face and back a bit. The push snap is identical to the regular front snap kick except instead of striking and returning, you thrust out and

IN THE FRONT PUSH SNAP KICK, THE LEG COMES UP AS THE TOES CURL BACK TOWARD YOU.

push forward with your hips to shove him back with your foot. This is not to say that the push kick is merely a moving device; it's still a good, hard kick to the stomach, but if you throw your hips and body weight into the move, you can knock your opponent back a few steps and create some breathing room.

THE PUSH SNAP KICK RELIES ON YOUR HEEL AND YOUR BODY WEIGHT TO SHOVE YOUR OPPONENT BACK.

• *The knife edge kick.* No bloody steel involved here, just a different foot position from beginning to end. For the knife edge kick, you strike with the "bladed" side edge of your foot.

To get into the correct position to shoot this kick, you need to stand sideways to your opponent. You can't make this movement by facing him and trying to twist your hip and foot into this edged position. Either strike him with the foot that is closest to him or cross over and hit him with your rear or trailing foot. In either case, pull your toes toward you and let the bladed edge of your foot—backed with your forward momentum and body weight—do all of the damage.

The knife edge kick has one simple target—your attacker's knee joint. After tinkering with this kick for awhile, you'll find that the edge of your foot fits perfectly into the side of your attacker's locked knee joint. By striking this vulnerable spot and driving through the target just like you do for fist blows, you can cause a "buckling" sensation that will cripple your assailant.

THE KNIFE EDGE KICK IS PERFECT FOR BREAKING KNEECAPS.

And just like the front snap kick, you can repeatedly throw the knife edge kick to his knee as often as it takes to end the confrontation. Kick to one side of his knee and then aim for the other side. Switch targets and attack the other knee. You're bound to put him on the ground because, as the old saying goes, "A house built without a foundation will surely fall."

Some fighters like to use the knife edge kick from the side that faces their opponent. Here, they just pick up their close leg, cock it slightly, and drive it into the knee. This close-quarters kick is excellent when you feel jammed by your attacker or you want to initiate a fight-ending strike as he steps toward you.

Other fighters prefer to "wind up" their knife edge kick by crossing over and using their trailing leg to strike with. This gives more power to the kick and it also helps close the gap between you and your opponent if you are too far away to hit him with your fists.

Using a slightly split stance, bring your rear leg forward and into the knife edge bladed position as you pivot on your toes and twist your front hip and leg to the side. When you finish this kick, your front foot should be pointing almost behind you as you strike. From this position, you can throw another knife edge kick with the foot that is now closest to your assailant.

• *The front wheel kick.* This kick is another old favorite of martial artists and kick boxers. You can throw it from a number of positions and at a number of targets. How ever you throw or aim this kick, always remember to strike with the top flat part of your foot, just above the toes and below the ankle.

More than any other kick in this book, the wheel kick relies on hip pivot, hip torque, and hip position. If you plan to use this kick under any circumstances, get the foot and hip movements down first.

Like the knife edge kick, you can throw the wheel kick using the foot closest to your attacker (assuming you're in a boxer's stance already) or by using the trailing or rear leg. In either use, you must end up with your hip turned and your nonkicking foot facing *behind* you. After you practice the wheel kick, you'll notice how hard it is to fight your own body and *not* turn your hip and foot over.

Starting with the foot closest to your attacker, raise your leg to waist level, turn your foot inside so the top part becomes the striking area, and snap it out toward your opponent. At the same time, pivot slightly on your nonkicking or rear foot so that your toes face behind you and your hips *rotate* along with the rest of your leg as it moves. Done properly, you can use the front-foot wheel kick to strike your enemy in

THE FRONT WHEEL KICK IS PERFECT FOR MIDDLE AND UPPER B.E.A.T. TARGETS.

the knee joint, rib cage, abdomen and solar plexus, and even the side of the head.

The front-foot wheel kick is a fast-moving, high-impact kick that serves to knock your opponent down or out. A hard front-foot wheel kick to the knee will cripple him, a hard wheel to the ribs will double him over, and a hard wheel to the side of the face will turn out his lights.

While the front-foot wheel kick works well in many of the same circumstances as the front-foot knife edge kick, the rear leg wheel kick can be even more devastating. Since you have the time and distance to generate more speed with your leg, you can create much more pain and dysfunction for your attacker.

For this kick to work, remember to pivot your nonkicking foot and turn your hips. No pivot and no turn means no wheel kick. You'll find it much easier to execute this movement when you let your body go where it wants naturally, turning and sliding on your toes and feet to allow your hip to open up and pop the kick against the target.

REAR KICKS

Although the name suggests a boot to the butt, rear kicks actually refer to your rear-facing position with respect to your opponent. Whereas with front-facing kicks you attack while facing your enemy, with rear kicks you turn your body away from him and shoot your kicks behind you.

The beauty of rear kicks is that they confuse your attacker. When you turn your back on him and crouch slightly, you send a whole range of thoughts reeling through his head. If you listen carefully, you can hear the tiny wheels turning inside: "Why is his back to me? Is he turning to leave? Is he going to run away? Should I chase after him? What do I do now? He's messing up my one and only plan!"

While he is attempting to answer these questions, you will be aiming your butt at his body, bending slightly at the waist and looking over your right or left shoulder (depending on which foot you plan to use). If he gets within range—either by coming after you or if you're close enough—you can lift and cock your foot, not unlike a dog using a fire hydrant, and fire a rear kick into his abdomen.

KEY: In all uses, the rear kick uses the heel of your foot as the striking point. Keep your toes pointed down toward the ground and aim the bottom of your foot right at the place you want to strike. Then drive your bony heel right into your attacker and quickly pull it back. From this point, you can fire another rear kick into another location, switch to fist blows, or continue with other kicking movements.

This kick works especially well when he is really upset and coming after you with a vengeance. Imagine his surprise when you stop and jam your solid foot and powerful leg right into his gut as he comes near. Few "chasers" expect the "chasee" to stop and jam a foot into their belly or balls.

Rear kicks can get your attacker off your back, so to speak. If he is too close or moving too quickly in your general direction, drop into a crouch from your fighting stance, turn your back to him slightly, and shoot your leg into his body.

This kick works

THE REAR KICK PUTS YOUR HEEL INTO HIS BELLY.

even better if your opponent is kind enough to bend forward in an attempt to tackle you or grab you around the waist. If his head drops below your shoulder level, aim your rear kick upward and drive the heel of your foot into his chin or nose. You've effectively kicked him in the head without exposing the rest of your body to a counterattack.

This rear-facing movement also gives you an additional time and distance advantage should you feel the need to exit the area with all possible haste. Since you're already in a crouching position that resembles a sprinter in the starting blocks, you can capitalize on this low-to-the-ground stance and hightail it out of the fight zone should you think it necessary.

Like all the other offensive, assaulting fist and leg strikes in this book, the rear kick is equally useful with your right or left leg. The difference in how you use this important kick lies in the position of your feet before you throw it and, more importantly, which shoulder you look over to see your enemy's B.E.A.T. model targets.

(As a quick review, B.E.A.T. stands for BRAIN, EYES, ABDOMEN, TESTICLES. For kicking purposes, any of the targets in the head, sternum, and lower body can hurt your assailant enough to stop the fight.)

To throw a rear kick using your right leg, look over your right shoulder. To shoot a left leg rear kick, look over your left shoulder. This may sound painfully simple at first, but in the heat of battle it's easy to forget where and how to look at the target. Even championship pistol shooters can forget which eye to close or how many rounds they have left in their weapons during an exciting contest.

If you look over the opposite shoulder to execute the kick, you may miss your target because of a "cockeyed" approach. Remember, right rear kick means a right shoulder view and a left rear kick means a left shoulder view.

The starting and finishing points of your body are just as crucial as your view of the target. Try as you may, it's nearly impossible to shoot an effective, on-target rear kick from a completely vertical position. Unlike with more spontaneous kicks like the front snap and the front wheel, you must first get into position before the rear kick can go off smoothly. Further, you can't throw a rear kick from the front! Turn away from your opponent quickly, bend at the waist, look over the proper shoulder, and fire away.

Don't worry about "exposing your flanks" to your enemy as you throw this kick. You're placing an enormously powerful obstacle directly in his path—your leg and that bony knob on the end of your foot known as your heel.

Two Types of Rear Kicks

Rear kicks come in two shapes and sizes: shuffle rear kicks and crossing rear kicks. The kicks you choose depend on one distinct factor: distance. How close or far away you are from your assailant and how close or far away he is from you will tell you which one to choose.

The difference between the two kicks lies in the foot position and the distance you keep your kicking leg and your nonkicking leg apart:

• *Shuffle rear kicks.* With these you step toward your opponent by placing your feet even with each other. You start out in the rear kick position with your legs slightly split. Stepping toward your opponent, you bring both feet even with each other and shoot the rear kick. This one is useful if your attacker is already close to you or coming in toward you to strike.

• *Crossing rear kicks.* This kick covers a good amount of distance between you and your attacker. It's useful if he is backing away or you are too far to reach him with front fist blows or front kicks. Starting with your feet in the rear kick position, step *deeply* past your kicking foot with your stationary foot and move it about 3 feet in front of you. Before coming to a complete stop, shoot your kicking foot into your target. In one complete motion this almost looks like a charging rear kick; since you don't stop to strike, you can generate more

THE STARTING POSITION FOR A SHUFFLE REAR KICK. NOTE THE FEET ARE CLOSE TOGETHER.

momentum.

Remember that the differences between the two lie in the distance: shuffle rear kicks start when the feet come together and crossing rear kicks start when the feet have split apart. With each kick, the kicking foot moves toward the target all at once; there is no pause with either kick.

Like the others, practice these kicks in front of a full-length mirror and a heavy bag to get the distances down.

SPINNING KICKS

As much as I like to look at spinning kicks in the karate studio or on a movie screen, and as much

THE MIDDLE POSITION FOR A SHUFFLE REAR KICK. YOU MOVE A SHORT DISTANCE TO REACH YOUR OPPONENT.

as I like to do them during a practice session, they are, in a word, difficult. Difficult to teach, difficult to demonstrate, and difficult to practice repeatedly unless you have the inner ear balance of a space shuttle astronaut.

Before you worry that you'll never master such a complicated once-around-your-body

FINISH WITH A HARD, ACCURATE ABDOMEN KICK.

THE STARTING POSITION FOR A CROSSING REAR KICK. YOUR FEET ARE FURTHER APART AS YOU STEP EVEN CLOSER.

technique, know first that the movement is amazingly similar to a spinning back knuckle, only you use your foot instead of your hand.

For all their inherent problems, spinning kicks do help you get your kicking momentum going. Anytime you can move your body at high speed and in a

complete circle, you will generate some effective force. And besides the clear fact that spinning kicks are difficult to do, they also have the reputation of being equivalent to a right roundhouse punch. In a word, spinning kicks are telegraphic. If your opponent has any fighting sense at all, he may realize a spinning kick is en

THE MIDDLE POSITION FOR A CROSSING REAR KICK. YOU'RE IN CLOSER THAN WITH A SHUFFLE REAR KICK.

route and be able to block it and punch your lights out.

Even the average street dummy may notice you spinning around like a kid's top and have sense enough to step aside or jump back in time to avoid the kick. But if you are quick enough and have some things going for

AGAIN, FINISH WITH A HARD, ACCURATE ABDOMEN KICK.

you like poor lighting, close or confining spaces, and a dimwitted assailant, you can use a spinning kick to your immediate advantage.

The movements for a spinning rear kick are similar to the movements made for a standard rear kick, save for one noticeable exception: in a spinning kick, you start in a split stance

YOU CAN START THE SPINNING REAR KICK MUCH FARTHER AWAY.

AFTER TURNING COMPLETELY AROUND (LIKE A SPINNING BACK FIST), YOU STRIKE WITH YOUR TRAILING LEG, JUST LIKE ANY REAR KICK.

and kick with your trailing or rear foot after you have turned completely around.

With a regular rear kick, you pivot forward and kick with the foot that is already facing your enemy. In a spinning move, you have to turn all the way around to kick with your rear leg.

KEY: Rear kicks

use the foot closest to the target; spinning rear kicks use the foot farthest from the target.

Look at the photos of the spinning rear kick and then start practicing. Remember to strike with your heel, and try not to get too dizzy while you work out the basics of this special foot technique.

FOOT FIGHTING TARGET AREAS

Now that you know *how* to kick, let's focus on *where* to kick your opponent. As with fist and hand blows (and good real estate investments), it's all a matter of location, location, location. Let's start from the top—at the head, assuming you're flexible enough to reach this area. If not, just kick what you can reach and practice and stretch until you can hit this inviting but high target.

• *High foot targets.* Aim for the sides of the head, the sides of jaws, the neck, or the ear holes. As always, keep your soft bony foot away from your opponent's hard bony forehead or the top of his skull. Use the flat top part of your foot to strike, and use all of your leg and body power to make this a knockout blow.

KEY: High kicks work best for long-legged, flexible fighters. A high kick puts you at risk if it's not done quickly and accurately. Watch your balance and hit what you aim at. If you can't do it safely, go lower.

In some instances, instead of bringing your foot to your assailant's head, bring your assailant's head to your foot. If you start with a hard front snap kick to the groin, you'll bend him over so you can easily kick his face. Don't bring the river to the donkey, bring the donkey to the river.

• *Middle foot targets.* The entire middle body area offers a number of inviting foot targets. Hit the side of his ribs using front wheel kicks; push a hard front push kick into his belly to gain some distance; throw a burning front snap kick into his abdomen; aim a solid rear kick deep into his stomach; drive a snap kick into his face as he bends from your first fist or foot blow. Finally, begin and end the fight with a single, well-placed, hard and fast, blood-draining snap kick to his testicles. As an experienced fighter

IF YOU HAVE THE HIP STRENGTH AND FLEXIBILITY, AIM YOUR FRONT WHEEL KICKS AT HIGH TARGETS.

once said, "You get a hard snap kick into his balls and the fight is over. It's over."

• *Lower foot targets.* There's nothing in the "Book of Rules" (which doesn't exist anyway) that says you have to actually make contact with the first kick you throw. Some of the best fighters in the world will fake with a kick 10-15 times before they ever throw it. By the time their opponent figures the fake is just a fake, BOOM!, in comes the real kick and this time it's packed with power.

Low targets like the knees, shins, and ankles serve as perfect fake-kick spots. If you fake like you're going to throw a low wheel kick to your attacker's knee and then jam that same wheel kick into his ribs, you'll certainly catch him off-guard. Further, you can fake a high wheel kick to his ribs and then go down and blast his knee joint with the same hard wheel kick. You don't always have to hit skin and bone with everything you throw. Fake a movement and change targets, or fake with a kick to one side of your assailant's body and then hit him on the exact opposite side with your other foot.

Use your knife edge kicks to damage and break his knees. Use your heel to stomp on the back of his Achilles tendon if you get behind him. Stomp on his shin bone, just a few inches below his knee and "rake" the edge of your hard-soled shoes downward across this delicate bone and painfully thin skin.

Whether you kick primarily low or high depends upon your body type, the height and weight of your attacker, how much room you have to fight in, lighting and street conditions, and even the weather. I wouldn't suggest a spinning rear kick to the abdomen if you're trapped against a building with your opponent while standing on an icy piece of black asphalt in the middle of the night. Think before you move and then go all out. Your brain is by far your most powerful weapon.

Focus on good foot positions from beginning to end, see your target before and after you strike it, and look at the "big picture" to tell you what to do first, next, and last.

Don't just hit what you're aiming at; hit *through* it. Set yourself up before you move. If you plan to throw a front snap kick, you had better face your attacker and prepare to drive forward with your rear leg. If you want to use a wheel kick to hammer his ribs, get your foot turned over, rotate your hips, and point your nonkicking foot backward. If a rear kick to the abdomen is what you want, point your butt at the target, look over your shoulder, and drive your heel into the spot as you point your toes down.

Concentrate on accuracy first and speed will mysteriously arrive after you've shown yourself you can hit what you aim for. If you miss, kick again or try something else with your hands. Don't hesitate to use two- and three-kick combinations, two- and three-punch combinations, and, best of all, kick-punch combinations. Follow up whatever you do with something else, whether it works the first time or not.

GROUND FIGHTING

Experience and a critical eye tell us that a high percentage of streetfights end up with one or both parties on the deck, scrabbling at each other like crabs in a pot.

Under no circumstances—unless you're an Olympic-caliber wrestler or have participated in "WrestleMania 13"—do you want to go to the ground intentionally with some urban guerilla bent on giving you major doses of harm and grief. The ground is an unforgiving place, and should you happen to linger there for even longer than 10 seconds, you could receive a body-beating even General Custer would shake his head at.

Human beings are meant to walk around vertically. We are out of our element on the ground and, as a rule, we have very little experience fighting from this vulnerable position. And yet, it happens.

But as bad as the ground is for you, it's a terrific place to not-so-gently put your attacker. If you can get him off his feet while you keep yours, the encounter changes dramatically to your favor.

If you both happen to end up on the ground, here are some tips that may help you escape:

• As fast as you can spin on your side or butt, get your feet up next to your assailant's head. With your feet up by his melon, it's much easier to kick him there.

• Use your leg muscles—the largest and most powerful in our body—to kick and kick and kick until you've knocked him out cold.

• If you can't kick at him, at least get on your feet as fast as possible. You may be able to catch him with a hard punch or kick as he tries to get on his feet after you.

• If you're trapped on the ground, don't just lay there. Keep moving! Spin, slide, twist, scream, and yell, but don't come to a complete stop. It's much harder to hit a moving target.

• If your assailant gets up before you do, sit up into a

"lever" position—on your butt, palms flat on the ground to support your weight, one or both legs in the air—and use your hands and feet to spin like a child's top. By pivoting around, you can follow his movements and fight him off with your feet until you can get up safely.

• If you can get to your feet before him,

SPIN AROUND TO PUT YOUR FEET NEXT TO HIS HEAD.

push him back over each time he tries to get up. Use this opportunity to save your energy and catch your breath. Shove him back down each time he comes to three-point or four-point stance. He'll soon learn how draining it is to pull himself up to a complete stand-ing stance time after time.

YOU CAN FIGHT EFFECTIVELY ON THE GROUND BY USING ONE OR BOTH FEET.

• Once you've turned the tables and kept him on the ground, go after the same B.E.A.T. model targets as you would if our attacker were on his feet. Kick to his head, face, abdomen, and testicles to your heart's content. Batter his jaw, ribs, and balls with your best snap kicks. Stomp heavily on his head, side of the neck, kidneys, back of the knees or Achilles heel. Stomp on his testicles if he is facing up or happens to roll over. Kick hard and often, but don't ever let him grab either of your feet or pants legs in an effort to pin you.

The longer the fight lasts, the more chances you have to break Newton's Law of Gravity, so that one or both of you ends up on the ground. Fight tactically, keep your balance, and, most importantly, know when to break free from touching your enemy while you're still in a vertical position of safety. Holding on for dear life as you ride this guy to the hard deck is a good way to leave pieces of your body where they don't belong.

A FOOT NOTE

In all kicking movements—the front snap and the knife edge, the front wheel, the rear kick, and the spinning kicks—it's all a matter of hip and foot movements. There are really only three parts: the ready position, the half-way position, and the finished position. While it is three separate movements blended together, a breakdown along the way with any of these critical moves and the kick probably will fail.

• *The ready position.* First things first. Get your hands up in front of your face! I see too many fighters concentrate so hard on their kicks that they forget to protect their faces. Consequently, when the kick fails or it takes them too close to their attackers, they get popped in the face because their hands are hanging unused by their sides. Start any kick just like you would a hand or fist movement—with your mitts up in the air, in front of your face, and ready to block any incoming blows.

Once your hands are in position, move your body and

your feet to get them into position. With front snap kicks, for example, put your kicking leg slightly back and bend a bit at the knees. Make sure your feet are facing forward and your kicking foot is ready for the impact that will follow.

• *The half-way position.* By now, you're well into the kicking movement and just about to hit your target area. During a front wheel kick, your hips should be "turned over," your nonkicking foot should be pointing nearly behind you, and your kicking foot should be taut and flexed into the proper position for impact. Your eyes should be open and looking not just at your target but at your assailant's whole body. Your mind and body should be ready for the hard snapping impact to come.

For all your kicks, excellent foot position will protect your toes and foot bones from harm and deliver more force to the kick. To shoot hard knife edge kicks, use the bladed edge of your foot. Curl your toes and pull your ankle back slightly to focus your energies on your foot's hardened edge. For rear kicks, make sure your body is bent at the waist and your toes are pointing straight down to the ground. And for your spinning movements, it's critical that you keep your eye on your opponent and on your kicking target to avoid that whooshing "air ball" feeling if you kick and hit only the breeze.

• *The finished position.* Here's where a number of potentially good kicking fighters fall down on the job. Many people slip into the bad habit of letting their kicks "drop" after they've used them. Instead of snapping their legs and feet back to the original "ready" position in preparation for another one, they let their legs fall forward like wounded ducks crashing into a pond. The primary danger here, besides the fact that it usually puts you too close to your opponent and his fists and feet, is that you suddenly aren't in a very good position to attack your enemy again. Don't let this happen to you. Snap your legs out and back, pausing only to strike the target before heading back home.

This "falling forward" effect can leave you flat-footed and vulnerable if the first kicking blow didn't put your opponent down. Besides the fact that it's bad form and looks awful, it violates the "Ready-Set-Go" principles I've tried to drill home throughout the book. Shoot your kicks out and back and get ready for another one, just as if the first one never happened. You may not need to throw it again, but if you do, you'll notice you're already in position for it to come out.

KEY: Do what is fastest, what you remember best, and what will get the job done under the circumstances. Train for what you know and keep your strengths and limitations in mind. If you're light and limber, kick high and hard to the head. If you're sturdy and not so flexible, kick to the knees and ribs. All of those fancy spinning kicks you see in martial arts movies are the result of hours and years of practice. If you can do those, great; if not, stay within yourself and work on more practical kicking movements.

CHAPTER 6

Pressure Point Nerves

"Illegitimi non carborundum"
("Don't let the bastards grind
you down.")

—Anonymous

If you're harboring any feelings that this chapter will teach you the proper way to use the now-famous "Mr. Spock's Vulcan Death Hold," sorry to burst your bubble. You may be able to find a book that offers specific instructions on this valuable fighting tool in the science-fiction aisle at your local bookstore. Or you may want to rent one of the many *Star Trek* movies now out on video and see if you can pick up a few hand-to-nerve pointers yourself.

While this chapter focuses on more realistic nerve-pinching movements, the Spock grip is not without its basis in fact. You actually *can* make someone curl up into a convulsive, whining ball of jelly if you know how and where to grab or hit him, how much pressure to exert, and when to let go or back away from your prey.

To understand how to use pressure point nerves and nerve roots to your advantage in the street, you'll first need to understand a bit of human physiology. Your central nervous system is just like the electrical wires that control and power parts of the engine in your car. When all systems are running normally, your car idles smoothly and can accelerate away from the curb when you hit the gas pedal.

But if you could take an imaginary pair of pliers and tightly squeeze one of the spark plug wires, you'd certainly notice a marked difference in the way your engine functioned. If you could squeeze hard enough to block the electric signals (or impulses) that flowed to the spark plug chamber, you would significantly reduce your engine's power. And if you unhooked a spark plug wire, you could shut off your engine's electrical supply completely.

Your body's nervous system works in a similar albeit much more sophisticated way. If you block a nerve impulse that surrounds your large muscles, you create the same type of dysfunction as you would if you squeezed a spark plug wire with a pair of pliers.

Your nerves run like rivers, firing millions of "movement" signals into your muscles and all in a fraction of a second. Throw a few big logs into these rivers and you'll quickly dam up the works. Hammer your opponent on top of one of his major nerve centers—also known as "pressure points"—and you'll shut down his nerve river just as quickly.

Fortunately for you, it's not necessary to be a trained neurologist to either find or interrupt your opponent's major nerve lines and centers. The human body houses over 350 potential pressure points, and most of them lie just under the surface of the skin. You can hit the main ones with your fingers, fists, palms, or feet. With some practice and a little practical knowledge of the human anatomy, you can add pressure point assaults to your fighting knowledge.

But as the old saying goes, "A little knowledge is dangerous." If you choose to strike potential pressure point areas on your attacker, you had better decide now and forever to do it hard enough to do the job correctly the first time. If you miss the vital spot or hit with all of the enthusiasm of a wet blanket, then you probably won't get the desired crippling effect. Worse yet, you'll probably just enrage your opponent and bring on more control problems.

Of those 350-plus potential pressure points, only a handful should concern you. There are a few key spots hiding on your enemy's face, arms, and legs that you can attack with vigor. Using the proper fist or leg blow, enough pressure on the right location, and some luck, you can generate a double dose of pain. This "two-for-one" shot occurs because pressure point blows create pain *and* a loss of motor control in the area struck. This means that not only will your enemy feel the impact of your fist or foot strike, but he'll also lose temporary control of his muscles in and around that site.

For years, police officers and skilled martial artists have used pressure point holds to get control of unruly people by creating "pain compliance." The difference for you lies in how you attack your assailant's pressure points.

Unlike the cops, who do this sort of thing for a living, you shouldn't be concerned with pain compliance—gripping, twisting, and joint-bending techniques that cause unarmed people to give up and go along with the program. You don't have the same civil responsibility to protect street jerks from themselves by not injuring them unnecessarily during high-risk arrest confrontations.

Since you're not bound by the same civil or criminal hindrances, you can attack these places with the intent to stop the fight quickly and get some street urchin out of your way. The pressure point techniques that follow were specifically created to help you generate maximum pain for your attacker in the shortest amount of time. If you can hit him in such a way that he can no longer use his brain, arms, or legs, at least for a few precious seconds, then you have effectively created an opportunity to escape untouched.

The best thing about using pressure points as a fighting tool is that nearly anyone can use them. Since the nerve areas you're interested in lie just below the surface of the skin, it takes only one or two foot-pounds of pressure (less than needed to pull the trigger of a gun) to reach them.

KEY: Large muscles and extra body weight aren't necessary for good pressure point attacks. Fingers, fists, and feet will do the job just fine. Review the following pressure point sites and (gently) test your accuracy by finding them on your own body. Then (gently) test them on a willing partner to see if you can locate them effectively. Once you know how to find them with your fingers, start practicing your fist and feet blows to hit these target areas. Using a heavy bag or a full-length mirror should help you improve your accuracy.

Commit the following sites to memory and aim for them each time you strike your attacker:
• *Under the nose.* Aim for the area just below your attacker's nose and just above his upper lip. If he has a mustache, center your blow right on the spot where his facial hair starts to appear under his nose. Any pressure to the infraorbital nerve that lies directly in this site will bring tears to the eyes of even the toughest men. For best results, try to strike in a slightly upward manner here.

You can hit this spot using a number

PUSH UP AND BACK, DRIVING YOUR KNUCKLES INTO THE BONY AREA ABOVE THE LIP.

of hand positions, including right or left chops using the bladed edge of your hand to drive up and into the target; a hard palm strike that rams the heel of your hand upward toward the top of his head; a ridge hand using the bony area at the base of your index finger and above the webbing of your thumb; and last and certainly best, you can accurately place a half-fist blow right into this point.

To hit right on the nerve by grinding the bone above the upper lip with your half-fist knuckles, pull back your attacker's head by grabbing his hair and pop him right on the bone. One strike to this sensitive point will cause brain-rattling, eye-watering pain.

• *Under the ear.* The area behind your ear and where your jawbone ends is rich with nerves. Even slight pressure to this spot—known as the mandibular angle—can send pain sensations shooting throughout your attacker's head, face, and rear skull. Using a hard fist blow, a chop, or a hammer fist to hit this delicate spot will send shock waves into your enemy that will stun him at the least and put him out at the best. Use your own thumb to probe for this spot and push upward toward the top of your head until you feel the need to say "uncle."

STRIKE THE NECK JUST BELOW THE EAR. USE THE TOP OF YOUR FIST TO DIG IT IN.

Reaching this area is easier if you are slightly off to the side of your opponent. If you can stand facing his side while he's looking forward, you should have no trouble jamming a hard punch into this zone. You also can use the bottom of your fist to hammer at this spot. The harder you hit and the more times you reach the target, the more likely you will knock your opponent down and out.

• *Under the jaw.* The fleshy area in the middle of the under-side of your jaw— sometimes called the

USE A HARD SPEAR HAND TO DRIVE INTO THE FLESHY UNDERSIDE OF THE JAW.

"soft" palate—covers the hypoglossal nerve that connects to the back of your tongue. While this area may be hard to reach on a moving target, you can cause intense pain by poking at a middle spot, just inside the under part of the jaw and between the end of the jawbone and the jaw point at the beginning.

A hard poke with the fingers—like a spear hand or an eye shot, but drilled directly into the skin—will reach this area best. An uppercut punch using the first two knuckles also will cause some damage. You can even try to use the point of your thumb as a battering ram. Hit this spot only when you feel very comfortable that you can be accurate with a blow; otherwise, try to reach under his nose or under his ear first.

• *The forearm nerve.* The radial nerve runs across the top of your forearm. A good place to hit it lies in the thinly muscled area between your wrist and your elbow. Lift your wrist up as you look at the top of your forearm. Find the natural crease heading more toward your elbow and press

SLAM A HARD CHOP ONTO HIS FOREARM NERVE.

your thumb right into the middle. You should feel the nerve give off "ouch" signals when you probe at it.

This pressure point controls the movement of your attacker's hand and wrist. If he makes the mistake of grabbing you, just hammer a hard open-hand chop straight down on top of this nerve point. Or hit hard with a downward hammer fist and try to split his forearm muscle into two pieces. The shock waves you send with this forearm blow will loosen his grip and make him yelp in pain as his arm throbs from wrist to elbow. Follow up with a fist or a foot blow and end the confrontation.

The secret to this pressure point, as with all the others, is to strike hard, hard, hard! No little love taps will do. You must use sufficient force to create dysfunction in your opponent's brain or appendages.

And this time, instead of trying to drive through the opponent, let your fist and foot blows *linger* a bit on the target areas. This extra split second of impact will help add more shock to the force of the blow. But don't keep your hands or feet on these spots forever unless you want your attacker to make a grab for you. Just let the impact of the blow travel through your opponent's nervous system by maintaining contact with his body for a bit longer than normal.

• *Side of the thigh.* You'll find another tender nerve point about 4 inches above your kneecap on the side of your thigh. A sharp, well-placed right or left wheel kick here can send your attacker stumbling to the ground. Like with your fist blows, let your kick to this area dig in a bit and help displace more energy across the nerve site. If you hit this nerve correctly, you can cause pain in *both* of your attacker's legs and he will have no option

TRY TO DIG YOUR TOES INTO HIS THIGH.

but to take a hard seat on the pavement.

Some skilled martial artists have learned to use their own shin bones as a thigh-beating weapon, happily pounding at their opponent's outer thigh with a whipping wheel kick that slams bone against flesh. The impact from the shin bone wheel kick—if you can take the pain it produces in you—acts just a like a police baton blow to this area.

• *The top of the calf muscle.* You also can direct a hard-placed wheel kick to the side and back of your attacker's calf muscle. Even when facing him, you can still snake the top of your foot around the back of his leg using the wheel kick. If you aim at a spot just below the back of the knee and on the top of the calf, you'll hit his tibial nerve with the bony part of your foot. Like the thigh muscle pressure point, this one also will send him to the ground if you hit on target.

The calf is a dense, hard-to-develop muscle group. Even champion bodybuilders wail and scream about how difficult it

is to grow a healthy-looking set of calves. You've probably seen a host of "muscleheads" running around town in short pants. A fair number of these well-built bruisers will have calves shaped like small Christmas tree bulbs.

When it comes down to calf growth, good genetics are more necessary than 1,000 calf raises with 200 pounds strapped across your shoul-

SLAM HIS CALF WITH YOUR FOOT. IT WILL KNOCK HIM DOWN AND HIT THE CALF NERVE.

ders. I've seen a number of prison cons and parolees built like bulldozers—all from the waist up. What they had in 19-inch biceps and thick necks, they lost with 13-inch calves.

Use this information to your advantage. In my experience, the guys who spend all their days and nights working on their upper-body development usually dog it when it comes to the calves. That tibial nerve running the length of their skinny calves is just waiting to be kicked.

The secret to pressure point penetration is getting (your) bone on (their) nerve. To work effectively, your fist blows and kicks must penetrate deep into the target. Glancing blows, mis-hits, or strikes to targets in the general vicinity of the pressure point area may stop your attacker, cause him injury, or even end the fight, but if you can really reach deep with your blows, down past the skin, under the muscles and tissues, and into his nerve endings, you will be able to totally incapacitate your enemy.

Pressure-point fighting is like swimming during a rainstorm—you're going to get wet anyway, so why not enjoy yourself? In a streetfight, you'll have to hit him with a fist or foot blow anyway, so why not cause him total muscle and mental dysfunction as you do?

One final aside to the subject of pressure-point fighting tactics: the damage you inflict during a street confrontation should serve one purpose—to get the attacker off of you and out of commission as soon as possible. You don't want to have to deal with him longer than is absolutely necessary.

"Hit and split" has been the credo of this book. Attacking pressure points will not only help you serve that purpose, but it also will cause that son of a bitch to remember who you were and what you did to him. No joke. Pressure point pain can be hideous, causing even the most drunk or drugged-up idiot to take a hard seat, willing to do anything to make his nerve endings stop screaming.

KEY: If you can reach these targets and hit them hard enough to stimulate the required nerve endings, he will never, ever forget his encounter with you.

CHAPTER 7

Movement and Positioning

"When you win, nothing hurts."
—Joe Namath

Let's face it, some of us—present company included—are not exactly light on our feet. If you're what is politely known as "large-boned" or you don't have the instinctive rooftop-leaping reactions of an 18-year-old cat burglar, then this may apply to you. If you are thin and wiry or blessed with the proper combination of slow and fast twitch muscle fibers, then you may be built for speed.

But if the phrases "nimble as a gazelle" or "fast as a cheetah" won't apply to you anytime soon, fear not. The trick to being fast in a streetfight doesn't always have to do with blurring foot or hand speed, although it helps.

Surviving a fight calls for you to hit before you get hit, move before your assailant moves, and block or, better yet, avoid whatever comes your way. If you can do all of them, you'll walk away unhurt and victorious. But if you can only pick two, choose to focus on the first strategy and the last—hit first and stay clear of incoming blows.

Your enemy expects you to

fight like he does—in and out, forward and back, punching and grabbing whenever one of you gets close to the other. Even the slightest deviation from this plan can throw him off-stride and give you that split-second edge you need to hammer him and leave.

Although it's somewhat dangerous to generalize when it comes to your health and safety, if you assume that most people are right-handed and right-footed, the majority of punches are going to come at you from his right body area to your mirror image, or left body area. A right hook would hit the left side of your jaw, a left jab would hit your right eye, and a right wheel kick would attack the left side of your rib cage.

With this knowledge of positions and directions of attack in mind, it becomes much easier to *anticipate* your assailant's movements and decide not to be standing in the "strike zone" when his blow arrives. That's where the concepts of lateral movement and parrying come in to play.

Instead of always moving in and out and forward and back as you fight, move *laterally* or sideways away from your opponent. Just like a bullet fired from a handgun will miss its target if the shooter jerks the gun even an inch, with lateral movement it doesn't matter how much the punch misses you—1 inch or 1 foot—as long as it does. Don't get overly concerned about jumping 10 feet out of the way. Get used to making slight, lightning-quick adjustment moves that take you out of his striking range.

If your attacker throws a right punch aimed at your jaw, move quickly to your hard left and let it whistle past your right ear. While he's busy trying to regroup and figure out why you weren't on the receiving end, strike back!

If he aims a kick to the left side of your ribs, move hard to the right and watch as the kick comes full-circle and he loses his footing and falls on the ground.

If you aren't there to absorb the blow, it's likely the average street hood—who's used to getting his way after a single punch to his victim's face—will swipe helplessly at the air and not know what to do to recover his balance or his lost energy in time to avoid the rapid-fire series of blows you'll deliver next.

Practice lateral movements by moving your feet from side to side, rather than across each other. Besides being too slow, crossing your feet places you in an awkward position and makes you vulnerable to being tripped or shoved down. Don't let your legs get tied up. Move in half-steps to the side, letting your inside ankle bones come close to touching each other before you quickly move to the left or right.

Besides this side-step movement, don't be afraid to try the "bullfighter-Ole!" move, which simply calls for you to step aside quickly to the left or right and let your opponent go past you. Many martial artists skilled in aikido and judo always seem to end up behind their attackers as they go charging past and end up on the ground, usually thanks to a carefully placed foot or a grab-the-jacket-and-shove maneuver. These techniques work best with an aggressive opponent who rushes in toward you. If you have the room, side-step out of harm's way and let him kiss the street.

The key to effective lateral movements lies in knowing when and where to step to get out of the way. You can get information by reading your opponent's movements. Does it look like he wants to rush in and grab you? Is he winding up to give you a roundhouse right to the head? Will he try to kick you?

If it looks like he's going to try for the first fight-ending blow (which is your strategy), base your movements on avoiding him with lateral side-steps and hitting him first. And even if all else fails, taking only some of his blow is better than getting all of it flush. Keep in mind that he has to expend the same amount of energy to swing and miss you as he does to swing and hit you. Lateral movements burn very few calories for you. Make him use his endurance swinging at the empty air while you go where he is not.

PARRYING

Parrying movements—where you block or push away his punches or kicks as they come near—serve two purposes: to avoid or lessen the damage of your enemy's moves, and to put you in the right position to retaliate immediately with a punch or kick of your own. No matter how you do it—either by stepping laterally out of the way, guiding the punch past your head as you move, or batting a kick down as it comes in—try to get your hands out in front of you to repel his strikes. And once you do succeed in lessening the impact, hit him hard!

Too many fighters do one thing but not the other. They can punch hard but only after they let their attacker in to rain down his own blows. Other fighters can skillfully parry or avoid a blow, but they don't know how to step up and finish the fight. Instead of punching or kicking their enemy into submission, they continue to dance around their opponent, waiting for his next move.

The word "parry" means "to ward off a thrust or a blow" and takes its origins from the art of combat fencing. The best way to avoid a punch, besides helping it miss you altogether, lies in your ability to block it or send it in another direction. To accomplish either, you'll have to get close to your attacker, into his "inside" position. If you're so far away that his punches or kicks miss you already, then parrying is obviously not necessary. But if you're in jeopardy of receiving a "lamp job," you'll need to get in tight where you can use your forearms and elbows to block punches and kicks and your hands to push them off target. Here are two of the easiest methods to use in a pinch:

• *Advance and parry.* Step toward your opponent and block his first strike with your forearms and elbows or push it away with your hands. Once you're "on his inside," counterattack with fist, elbow, or chopping blows.

• *Retreat and parry.* Step away and to the side before you

block his strike or push it off target. Get his body—meaning his hands and feet—out of range so that he would have to move more than just a few steps in order to reach you again. Once his energy has been deflected with your countermovements, step in and attack with hands and feet.

Always remember to move your *head*

STEP INTO YOUR OPPONENT'S BLOW AND PUSH IT AWAY. BE READY TO RETALIATE.

first and your body second. You probably can stand a blow to the body, but you may not recover from a hard one to the head. Get your melon out of the way of any threat that comes toward you.

Use lateral movements to get yourself out of the path of the blow and then quickly counterattack. This

STEP AWAY FROM YOUR OPPONENT'S BLOW AND PUSH IT AWAY. THIS CREATES MORE ROOM FOR YOU.

helps to confuse your enemy as he wonders why his blow didn't work and why he now has to defend himself against your attack.

If you just can't avoid a blow, use your hands and large muscle areas to block punches and kicks and let your shoulders or thighs absorb most of the impact. Keep your mouth closed to avoid a broken jaw and try to anticipate the impact by tensing your muscles, especially around your abdomen.

A solid parrying push will deflect his energy and wreck his concentration. If you think it will help, scream as you do it to distract him and gather your adrenaline before you launch your own attack.

Keep your balance and help him lose his. Send him to the pavement with a push, a sweep, or a trip. Use your hands to pull his hair, grab his jacket, and get him into immediate pain on the hard ground.

Always move where he's not, where he doesn't expect you to be, and out of range. Move into range only to retaliate. You may not even need to use these parrying techniques if you follow the basic idea of this book: stop his force with your force first.

CHAPTER 8

Hand, Wrist, and Finger Strength Training

"And I will show you something different from either

Your shadow at morning striding behind you

Or your shadow at evening rising to meet you;

I will show you fear in a handful of dust."

—T.S. Eliot

Unless you plan to talk your way out of a potential fight situation or you have the body size or old-fashioned moxie necessary to intimidate your enemy, better plan on using your fists to solve the situation. If you can get out of a street encounter by outwitting some thug—which isn't particularly difficult—go for it. Any time you can avoid violence is a plus. Putting "hands on" can be a dangerous and difficult way to spend an evening.

But if words or appearance won't protect you, let your hands and feet do their work. Just like an auto mechanic or a plumber needs good tools to get the job done, so will you. Mental toughness, street savvy, and an aggressive attitude can only take you so far if you don't have the weapons to back up your vocal cords or experience.

Although it helps, pure size is

not always a distinct advantage. I've seen guys no taller than 5'4" outwit much larger opponents just by their sheer physical presence. Though they might appear small, some short men can strike fear into the hearts of street bullies just by staring hard at them.

Of course, it goes both ways. I've watched street hoods scan a crowd and head directly for the weakest target they could identify—usually a woman or a small or slightly built man. And I remember a story about a giant of a man who cleared out an entire bar just by walking in, placing a boxer's rubber mouthpiece between his lips, and announcing, "All right! Who's first?" between clenched teeth.

So while you can't change your height, and it takes months to change your body weight in either direction, you can "harden" your built-in weapons, starting with your hands.

The benefits to stronger hands, wrists, and fingers are twofold: you can hit harder, and you will protect these bony areas from injury. After all, who cares if you win the fight if you end up at the orthopedics section of the hospital emergency room anyway?

FIST EXERCISES

Most martial arts books and instructors will tell you to strike your opponent so that the first two knuckles on your punching hand make contact with the target. This advice is correct and has proved itself over countless years of fist fighting. But while these two joints are the largest in your hand, they are merely two of five (counting the thumb). Focusing your fist-strength training on exercises that develop and toughen only these first two takes away from your other joints. Since we know that fighting is an inexact science filled with many accidental moments, it makes more sense to train as if you were going to hit with the *whole* hand because technically, the whole hand is involved from beginning to end.

Having "tough fists" able to repeatedly deliver hard

punches is not a divine gift. It requires work, and since you weren't born with hands made from granite, you'll have to begin a program that conditions them for the possibility that you may need to deliver a future pounding.

Some people work in careers that build strong hands as a result of the work, including most construction trades, auto or heavy equipment repair, assembly-line work, and any other job that calls for heavy lifting, twisting, or holding with the hands. Other people active in martial arts, weight lifting, or boxing will tend to have hands that are thick and tough, callused in all the necessary spots, and able to take loads of abuse.

If you feel you need to improve the overall strength and sturdiness of your hands, consider the following hand exercise routine that emphasizes fist toughness:

• *Knuckle push-ups.* These are done just like regular gym class push-ups except you balance on your closed fists instead of your open palms. Start out by distributing your weight across the knuckles of your entire fist. As you get stronger and more used to the discomfort of this exercise, focus your weight across your first two knuckles only. Do as many as you can per day, breaking each set of knuckle push-up repetitions into several different sessions. Experienced martial artists do these knuckle push-ups by the hundreds. Start at 10 and go up by 10s until you can do 100 per day.

• *Fingertip push-ups.* Same principle as above, only now you use all four fingers and your thumb to balance your body weight in the push-up position. This exercise will give you tremendous hand strength, especially in the muscles and tendons around your palms and finger joints. Well-conditioned fighters can do these push-ups using just their four fingers without the thumb. Start with five repetitions using your fingers and thumb arched off the ground and work your way up to 25-50 per day. You can alternate these with knuckle push-ups for some variety.

• *Thumb push-ups.* A word of warning first: these push-ups—where only the thumb of each hand touches the floor—

KNUCKLE PUSH-UPS TOUGHEN YOUR ENTIRE UPPER BODY.

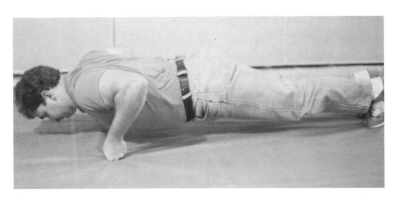

USE THE SAME GOOD FORM AS YOU WOULD FOR A REGULAR PUSH-UP.

are not for the novice. Don't even attempt them unless you've already put in hours of work on knuckle and fingertip push-ups first. Balancing on your thumbs alone—especially if you're heavy—can do more harm than good. With that caveat in mind, know that thumb push-ups are what separates the men from the boys. If you can crank out 10 of these ultimate

FINGERTIP PUSH-UPS TAKE GUTS AND WILLPOWER. DO AS MANY AS YOU CAN.

DISTRIBUTE YOUR WEIGHT EVENLY ACROSS YOUR WHOLE BODY. TRY TO RELAX YOUR HANDS.

toughies, your hands will have no problems in a streetfight. Start slow, use good form, and let any unnatural pains serve as a signal to stop.

• *One-handed push-ups.* For a quick review of how to do these correctly, go to your local video store and check out any of the early Sylvester Stallone *Rocky* movies. These one-

ONE-ARM PUSH-UPS TEACH YOU TO BALANCE YOUR BODY UNDER STRESS.

TRY TO CONCENTRATE ON A SMOOTH UP-AND-DOWN MOVEMENT.

handers really help your shoulder muscles develop, but since they place all of your body weight on one small area (your hand serves as a load-bearing tripod), they serve to strengthen your wrist, fingers, palm, and thumb. Use proper form, practice the balance portion first before you try one, then see if you can do 5-10 on each arm. You should feel this exercise

KNUCKLE BOARDS CAN BE PAINFUL AT FIRST. START SLOWLY AND BUILD UP.

work the muscles of your entire arm and shoulder.

• *Knuckle boards.* These devices are fairly controversial among sports medicine physicians, martial artists, and trainers. Fighters use these flat, square boards made of wood or, in some rare cases, cast iron to literally pound their fists into a toughened state. Some martial artists will cover the hard surface with bamboo, lines of thin rope, or cloth, and mount the board on the wall. Obviously, the amount of pounding you do relates to the existing condition of your hand. Using a knuckle board is like an uphill hike—you start slowly and build your self up as you go. One famous kung fu instructor in China was well known as "Iron Fist" because he carried his metal board around with him and pounded it for hours. Should you decide to use a knuckle board, start slowly, hit lightly with your first two knuckles, and gradually build up the time and intensity.

Having strong, tough fists can often mean the difference between a decisive victory and a bone-shattering loss. Genetics and the relative shape of your hands and fists should tell you which of these particular fist-building exercises will help you the most. If you already have hands shaped like horseshoes, you won't need to work nearly as hard as if you have hands that look like they were fashioned from wet breadsticks.

WRIST EXERCISES

Strong wrists are essential in any sport involving your hands. Whether you participate in ice curling or world-class arm wrestling, thick, solid wrists will always help your performance. Football, tennis, racquetball, golf, baseball, gymnastics, basketball, hockey—the list of wrist-applicable sports is nearly endless. With the notable exception of soccer, perhaps, few sports don't involve the wrists.

Weight lifting requires strong wrists in order to create that "line of strength" that runs down from the back of your knuckles and into your forearm. If you ever have the opportunity to watch champion powerlifters compete in the bench press, notice their thick wrists. The heavy weight across the bar rests on top of this wrist-forearm axis. Any bend in the wrist weakens the lifter's chances of success and, worse, promotes injuries.

Boxing, martial arts, and any punching activity require the same straight-line wrist technique. Punching with your wrists bent either up or down will surely signal the need for a hard plaster cast and weeks of therapy to rebuild your crushed hand bones.

Keep that wrist straight at all times. Imagine that you are wearing an immovable splint across your wrist and forearms, making it impossible to bend it. Transfer that image to your punches and keep your wrist straight if you plan to hit anything hard—a heavy boxing bag, a speed bag, or an attacker. Keep this good form in mind even if you're just "shadow boxing" with an imaginary opponent. Remember, train exactly the same as if it were a real threat situation.

You develop strong, straight wrists by choosing exercises that flex your fingers, strengthen your hands, and build your forearms. Here are some drills that help the first two:

• *Wrist rotations.* As deceptively simple as this exercise sounds—rotate your wrists clockwise and then counter-clockwise for 100 repetitions in each direction—it really helps to improve your wrist strength and overall flexibility. It involves your tendons, bones, and the area surrounding your wrist joint itself.

• *Squeeze! Squeeze! Squeeze!* There are dozens of wrist and forearm-strengthening devices on the market today. Some range from the absurd to the more practical, but in my opinion, few wrist devices work any better than a plain old rubber ball. Squeezing a racquetball, handball, or—if you have large hands to start—a tennis ball will quickly build the outside top of your forearm where it attaches to your biceps muscle. A few hundred repetitions spaced out over the day also will give you an oysterlike grip, useful for peeling people off of you or grabbing something that you want to stay grabbed, like hair or clothing.

If you get bored squeezing the ball, switch to those popular two-handled forearm "grippers." Or go to the toy store and buy three or four packages of putty and make your own squeezing "ball." If you want to get the same effect but at an even cheaper price, try making a ball out of crumpled aluminum foil and squeeze that until your hand gives out.

Besides the obvious benefits for your grip, wrist, and forearm development, squeezing is also a terrific time waster. You can get a good forearm workout while squeezing in your car, on a break at work, in front of the TV, or even lying in bed at night. The more repetitions you crush out, the better weapons your fists will become.

FOREARM EXERCISES

You already know you need to have strong wrists to hit

hard and spare yourself from injury. Strong forearms and strong wrists go together like pie and ice cream—each one makes the other better. You get strong wrists by having strong forearms and vice versa.

Besides more powerful punches and added wrist protection, bigger forearms just make it easy for you to do things like push-ups and hit the heavy boxing bag or your opponent's body. They also limit the chance of damage to your hand's muscles, bones, tendons, and ligaments.

Here are some tried and tested exercises to give you stronger, tougher forearms. You also may want to consult a reputable weight training book for more tips on growing a healthy set of forearms:

• *Barbell wrist curls.* Do this and the other classic forearm exercises while seated on the end of a sturdy bench. Grab a barbell at shoulder width and place your hands on top of your knees, palms facing up. Curl the bar for 12-15 repetitions, going for 3-4 sets and adding weight as you progress.

• *Barbell reverse wrist curls.* Same as the previous exercise except the palms should now face down. Cut the weight to a more manageable level and tough out 12-15 repetitions for 3-4 sets. Use good form and really make that underused top forearm muscle grow.

• *Dumbbell wrist curls.* Same position as barbell wrist curls except now you use a dumbbell. Start with a light weight and keep the palms up and the back of your hand firmly attached to your knee or thigh. Do 12-15 repetitions for up to 3-4 sets.

• *Dumbbell reverse wrist curls.* Same position, palms facing down. Use a light, light weight to help keep the form correct. Do 8-12 repetitions for up to 3-4 sets. Don't do too many of these unless your forearms are already in top shape.

• *Dumbbell wrist twists.* While standing, grab a light dumbbell in one hand. Holding it slightly palms out and away from your body, slowly twist it back and forth. You should feel this movement in your wrist and tendons too. Do both

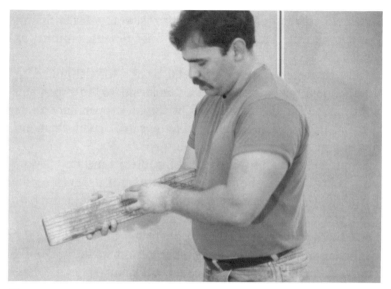

TAP YOUR OWN FINGER BOARD UNTIL YOUR FINGERS FEEL LIKE STEEL RODS.

sides for 8-12 repetitions. This is a good warm-down exercise to help round out your forearm weight-training routine.

FINGER EXERCISES

An old cynic once said, "The only thing that makes us different from dogs is that we have opposable thumbs."

Not only is this true from a physiological standpoint, but it also demonstrates why dogs are better biters than fighters. They can't grab their prey, at least for very long. We, on the other hand, can use our fingers and thumbs to grab, throw, push, parry, block, pinch, poke, stab, spear, claw, gouge, snatch, pull, lift, or move our enemies at will.

Besides the need for strong, tough hands, you'll also want to develop "quick" hands. If you can "reach out and touch" your enemy before he has a chance to react, you'll be able to initiate a number of fight-ending eye pokes, thumb shots, or spear hands to the abdomen. Don't hesitate to use your fingers to grab into the clothing and twist your assailant's soft flesh, especially around his neck, inner biceps, armpits, or testicle sack.

Just as there are wood or metal boards for fist-pounding development, you also can use a "finger board" to strengthen your digits. The design and the principles are similar except that for the finger board you strike repeatedly with the bony tips of your fingers, just under your nails.

Start slowly and gently and build up the intensity as your fingers toughen. A cast-iron metal frying pan works just as well as anything you could make or buy.

If you feel the need to further strengthen your fingers, go back to the finger and thumb push-ups described in the beginning of this chapter. Remember to start slowly and build your way up to solid, injury-free repetitions.

While you're practicing your squeezing repetitions in the car (keep one hand on the wheel!), at work, or at home, use that time to improve your hand positions too. Squeeze some grippers, putty, or a rubber ball, and practice your claw hands, finger eye pokes, and thumb eye pokes. How well you do it during your training and practice hours will reflect how well you react and perform the movement during those adrenaline-filled seconds before a streetfight.

If you have access to a heavy boxing bag, use it. Few things will better simulate the size and shape of your street attacker. Drilling your techniques on the heavy bag will help your brain and body coordinate with each other. The "muscle memory" you develop on the bag will transfer to real-life conditions when the time comes.

Most heavy bags weigh 40 to 70 pounds, but no matter the weight, you should always use cloth hand wraps and good quality boxing bag gloves to protect your hands. Don't think that wearing bag gloves isn't "macho." Even champion boxers wear bag gloves because they know how much protection they provide. Wear gloves, hit the bag softly at first and then build your intensity as your hand speed, timing, endurance, and coordination improve. Accuracy first, power later.

Besides improving your punching power, these simple exercises and drills harden the entire framework of your hands. What may appear obvious or simplistic on these pages could one day save you from broken hand bones. You'll need strong wrists, fingers, forearms, and knuckles in order to punch your opponent hard enough to make a difference.

If you can toughen these muscle fibers and tendons, you'll add power to your blows, increase the "shock absorbency" factor between your wrists and forearms, and protect yourself from injury should one of your punches veer off target and land on something hard.

CHAPTER 9

Leg, Hip, and Foot Strength Training

"Like men we'll face the murderous, cowardly pack,

Pressed to the wall, dying, but fighting back!"

—Claude McKay,
"If We Must Die"

During actor-comedian Steve Martin's rein as a "wild and crazy guy" during the late 1970s, he coined a term—"happy feet"—that certainly applies to your use of your own shoe-covered weapons during a streetfight. Martin's "happy feet" had him moving like a tap dancer possessed, all in one place, as fast as he could go.

"Happy feet," at least in our context, refers to your ability to move your hips, legs, and feet quickly enough to hit your target and withdraw. If you plan to use your feet to protect yourself in a street situation—as I have strongly recommended throughout the book—you must learn to control them. If you can't hit hard quickly and jump back quickly, you may cause more problems than if you just used your hands and fists.

Any time you raise your foot off the ground to kick your opponent, you put your balance in jeopardy. Few of us can stand around like flamingos all day, resting all our weight on one leg and one foot. Since we aren't built like camera tripods, this one-foot stance is subject to attack by our enemy. Even the slightest push or your own misstep can send you to the pavement in a hurry.

God help you if your attacker grabs your leg or foot after you attempt to kick him. With him holding your leg and you trying to stay upright, you suddenly lose everything you need to win the fight: the element of surprise, superior position, and the ability to strike first and strike repeatedly.

Worse yet, you also lose your chance to retreat. How can you back up or move laterally if you don't have both feet on the ground? If your assailant can seize your leg or foot, even briefly, he can turn the entire confrontation around. Don't let this happen! As I described in the chapter on foot fighting, kick hard and then pull your leg back with a quick snap. Be ready to fire off another kick to the same spot or choose another target. Or switch to fist or chopping blows and end the problem right there.

There is only one way to develop "quick feet"—practice constantly. The more kicks you can do on your own, either against a heavy boxing bag, in front of a full-length mirror, or just in the air during a "shadow box" routine, the better your kicks will become. Concentrate on good form first and let speed follow later. If you use the proper foot positions, high knee action, and a snapping out-and-back motion, you will have good kicks that are strong, fast, and accurate.

There is an old saying in martial arts: strong legs mean strong kicks and weak legs mean weak kicks. But too many new martial artists and fighters get hung up only the size of their leg muscles. There is much more to leg strength than mere muscle size. Hip strength, hip joint flexibility, hamstring and groin muscle flexibility, and hip power all contribute to overall leg strength. You can have each of these important ingredients and still have relatively thin leg muscles, depending upon your body type. And yet I've seen people with a healthy, well-built pair of legs who couldn't kick their way out of a wet paper bag. So don't always equate leg muscle size with leg strength.

All of this should tell you not to concern yourself with growing a pair of huge thigh muscles just to add more "oomph" to your kicks. Big, tree trunk-like thighs are nice to look at and will certainly add more power to your kicks, but they are not required to be a skilled foot fighter. Focus on developing speed and flexibility in your legs first. Muscle size is important to keep you healthy and injury-free, but try to think of it as just another dimension of your overall leg development.

Keep in mind that even Bruce Lee, possibly the most famous martial artist of our generation, did not possess mammoth leg muscles. His tremendous kicking ability came from years of practice that focused on excellent flexibility, kicking height, and foot position. Lee was a great kicker because he knew *how* to kick, not because he had huge legs.

KEY: Get used to kicking correctly first before you go for more speed, height, or power. If you use the proper foot position—i.e., toes pointed, toes curled back, edge of the foot pulled in, etc.—you won't have to worry about injuring your foot or breaking your toes. It's just like a professional football player knowing that the harder he tackles the less chance he has of injuring himself; it's only when he is tentative or tries to "ease up" that he runs the risk of hurting himself. And so it goes with kicks. If you're using the correct foot position and executing the kick properly, you'll have fewer problems than if you try to rush the movement in a sloppy fashion.

KEYS TO A HEALTHY LEG WORKOUT

To get your legs in shape and keep them there, you'll need to focus on the following key areas:

• *Muscle building.* You should tone and develop the large muscles of your legs, including your calves.

Almost any kind of lower-body resistive exercise you can think of will help to strengthen your legs. If you have access to a health club or gym, hit the leg extension and the leg curl machines to add size to your front thighs (quadriceps) and to your rear hamstrings. (If you're not sure how to perform these well-known exercises, consult a knowledgeable instructor or get one of the many good books on weight training from your local library or bookstore.)

When doing leg extension and leg curl exercises, keep the weight low and the number of repetitions high. You want to really strengthen both sides of your knee joint, so too much weight will only cause nasty muscle pulls or unnecessary strains. Try for 12-15 repetitions at a weight you can handle for at least three sets. Make sure you try to "lock out" your knee joints when doing front leg extensions and that you curl your leg all the way toward your butt during the leg curl movements.

With a high number of repetitions, you'll also put more of your heart and cardiovascular system into each exercise. Multiple reps tends to build your endurance more than two or three sets of six to eight reps. Remember, it's not size you're after right now, it's leg strength and joint and tendon flexibility.

Some people are fond of squats as the best lower body leg exercise. If you can stand the discomfort and have a strong, injury-free lower back, then squats can add size and power to your legs quite rapidly. If you can get to a gym with a squat rack or cage, have someone "spot" you to prevent any problems. Do the deep knee-bend squat exercise with a light weight first to get the form down, and then add repetitions and weight as your legs get stronger.

Most people unfamiliar with athletics tend to think of running as an exercise that causes you to lose weight rather than gain it. That's probably because people assume wrongly that a strict diet and a stern jogging program offers the only way to lose weight successfully. Further, many serious runners have relatively thin upper bodies, and this does little to dispel this "use it and lose it" philosophy.

But while running does burn calories, it serves as one of the best ways to build leg strength and size. Take a look at the average world-class sprinter and he or she will have tremendous lower (and usually upper) body development. Even champion marathon runners, who sometimes look as gaunt as prisoners of war, have well-defined thighs and calves.

The point is that you should not see running as just a way to melt off pounds but rather as a way to toughen and tighten your leg muscles. Running as little as three times per week will build your thighs and calves, strengthen your knee joints and the muscles, tendons, and ligaments that surround them, and tighten your ankle flexors and the ligaments in and around your toes. Each of these benefits, and the obvious cardiovascular help besides, will make you a better kicker.

After following a disciplined leg weight training and running program for a time, you should notice some significant improvements in your leg size and strength. All of these exercises will add to your kicking power as well.

• *Stretching and flexibility.* This is vital to avoid injuries, add height to your kicks, and increase the range of motion for your muscles, tendons, joints, and ligaments.

Now that you know how to build your legs, let's focus on what you'll need to know to lengthen your kicks, raise their height, and increase your distances. If you could choose between being born with great leg muscles or better than average flexibility, you should pick the latter. Big legs are handsome and intimidating, but imagine how good you'll feel if you have "bird legs" but can still kick a taller opponent square in the head! Flexibility, not muscle size, is what can do that for you.

There are two good ways to improve your leg flexibility. One is to practice kicking drills and movements over and over, and the other is to follow a good stretching program. Both are good, but the stretching program is often more practical and a more efficient use of your time than the kicking drills. To stretch, all you need is a padded surface,

THIS STRETCHES THE HAMSTRINGS.

THIS WILL LOOSEN YOUR QUADRICEPS.

THIS STRETCH WILL LOOSEN YOUR GROIN MUSCLES.

SWITCH SIDES AS YOU DO THIS INNER THIGH STRETCH.

such as a mat or the carpeted floor in your home. Kicking drills require enough space to move around and access to pads, a heavy bag, or, at the least, a full-length mirror. Stretching, on the other hand (or foot), takes up little room and can be done at home in front of the TV or before bed.

One of the key tenets to stretching is that it takes time. You can't expect to do splits after one month of work. Good martial artists stretch for years and years before they feel comfortable with their leg flexibility.

Before you begin any serious stretching program, study the available training tapes on the subject. Some of the best known martial artists (like Bill "Superfoot" Wallace, for example) have created stretching programs and offer them either in books or on videotapes. Locate one of these training aids and review it carefully before you begin.

The other key tenet to stretching is knowing your limits. If you have the lean, flexible body type that allows you to stretch long and hard, go for it. But if your body shape tends toward the heavy or muscular side, you'll need to work more slowly on your stretching techniques. Some people can bend at the waist and touch their heads to their kneecaps. Other people need weeks of stretching work before they can touch their fingers to their toes.

Since stretching has no time pressures, you can go at your own pace and follow the signals your body sends you. What you can do after one session may take someone else three weeks and vice versa. Keep your own goals as a streetfighter in mind and concentrate on avoiding injuries by stretching slowly and carefully. A single muscle pull, or worse, a tear, can set you back for months.

Set small, short-term goals and achieve them carefully. You'll want to spend most of your stretching time trying to improve your abdominal and hip flexor strength, your hip joint and socket flexibility, your lower back flexibility and rotation, your hamstring length and flexibility, and your inner thigh length and flexibility.

GOOD FOR A WARM DOWN, THIS EXERCISE LOOSENS YOUR LOWER BACK MUSCLES.

Don't push any stretching movement to the point of extreme pain. Stretching usually involves some discomfort, but you should never equate it with the "no pain-no gain" credo you see on those TV shoe commercials.

You'll know after a short time what feels good and what doesn't. Some stretching moves will seem as if they were designed specifically for your body and others you may not be able to complete. In any case, your body will tell you what area needs the most work.

• *Kicking power drills.* These are necessary to learn to be more explosive and powerful with your on-target kicks.

How you train at home or in a gym or studio is how you'll fight for real. The things you learn over and over again in the safety and comfort of a familiar training environment are the things that will save your ass in those dangerous streets.

To practice correctly and efficiently, you must get access to a bag or a mirror and a roomy place to train. A carpeted garage is good; a karate studio is better. The floor of an aerobics room is good; a boxing gym is better. Choose a location where you can train effectively without distractions.

Using either a heavy boxing bag or a full-length mirror to see your targets, go back and reread the chapters in this book on fist, hand, and foot blows. Review the B.E.A.T. model (BRAIN, EYES, ABDOMEN, TESTICLES), making sure you know where and how to hit your opponent. Develop a routine that works best for you, choosing the kicks that match your height and body style. Train yourself to move exactly as you would if it were a real-life combat situation. Teach yourself to kick in total darkness or with your eyes closed. It won't always be bright and sunny out there.

Try to make your kicks in close quarters, with your back against the wall, or blocked in on one or more sides. Practice your kicks from the ground, either seated or lying on your back. Drill with both legs and with both feet until you feel as comfortable with your strong side as you do with your weak side.

Each time you practice a kick, concentrate on going a little higher and kicking a little harder. In time, you'll raise your kicks from knee level to waist level to head level. All it takes is practice and a commitment to perfection.

KEY: Remember the important parts to any kick: the pre-kick movements where you get into position, draw back your knee, and cock your leg; the kicking movements, where you shoot your leg out and back, rotating or straightening your hip as necessary, and driving your foot into the target using the correct foot position; and finally, the post-kicking movements, where you pull back the kick, reposition yourself, and prepare to launch another blow or a combination of them.

In all cases, start slowly and let your power and speed build with your accuracy. It won't work in the streets if you can't do it in the training room first.

• *Foot position drills.* These will improve your foot and

ankle flexibility and help you focus on proper foot positions to avoid kicking injuries.

Like your stretching techniques, you can practice foot positions in front of the TV set. Lying on your side, you can execute each kick and focus on good toe and foot positions as you complete the three important kicking movements. To improve your "muscle memory" and learn the mental and physical images of each movement, try to "burn" the sensation of each kick and its proper foot position into your mind. Feel the snapping sound and let the start and stop of each kick pass through your muscles. Lock each kick out and strive to make small corrections as you aim for perfect kicks.

Since different kicks have different targets and rely on different foot positions, call out each kicking movement before you do it. Saying "right wheel kick to the ribs" will help you visualize the hip rotation, pointed-out toes, and top of the foot impact necessary to complete this kick safely and effectively.

The more you can do for your legs—by running, walking up many flights of stairs, weight training, stretching, or kicking—the stronger and higher you will kick. If you can build a powerful, flexible pair of legs, you can do significant damage to your attacker without injuring yourself. It's just like a professional baseball pitcher who knows that sturdy legs will help his arm propel the ball at 90-plus miles per hour. Leg muscles that are well-developed and still flexible will make your whole body tougher and able to work harder in a fight situation.

HOW TO FIGHT IN STREET CLOTHES

In the gym or at home, your workout wear probably consists of comfortable sweat pants or shorts and a cotton t-shirt. Even in a formal martial arts studio, you'll wear a cotton "gi" top with loose pants.

All of this sportswear should feel great, with no tightness or binding. Too bad it can't always be like that on the streets . . .

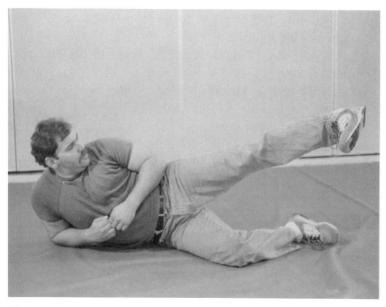

PRACTICE YOUR KNIFE-EDGE KICK FOOT POSITIONS FROM THE FLOOR.

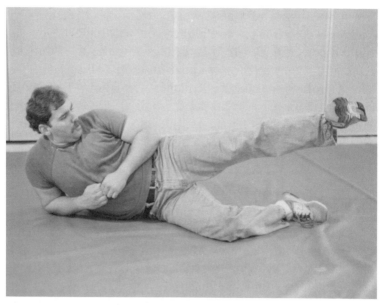

WORK ON YOUR SNAP AND WHEEL KICK FOOT POSITIONS LIKE THIS.

Walking home from work one cold, blustery night, you have your gloved hands stuffed deep into the pockets of your bulky down jacket. The part of your head that peeps out from your coat collar is covered with a wool knit cap. You're wearing heavy winter shoes and blue jeans. A man approaches you from a nearby stoop. It's clear he's not there to ask you the time and temperature . . .

Late for a business lunch, you pull your raincoat around your most expensive suit and huddle under an umbrella for the short walk to the restaurant. A man leaning against a parked car throws an insult your way. When you turn to look at him he pushes himself away from the car and gestures to you . . .

One warm summer night you and your date head out of the movie theater and start walking to your car parked a few blocks away. To get where you need to go, you must pass a noisy bar. A number of people have spilled out of the place and into the street. Someone in the crowd shoves you from behind as you go by. As you regain your balance, you see the man who did it start laughing . . .

What do each of these three street scenarios have in common? For one thing, there's a good possibility that a fight or at least the threat of a fight is about to happen. Each of the three men in these episodes is about to start "talking smack," to use an old streetfighting phrase.

And in each of these three, what you're wearing may have an enormous impact upon how you protect and defend yourself. The old adage "Clothes make the man" is true for fashion but may not work so well for streetfighting. Never let your desire to look fashionable dictate your safety. When you're out on the streets, choose simple, nonflashy clothes that offer you either freedom of movement (loose shirts and pants) or the best protection from blows (bulky winter jackets and heavy shoes).

What you put on your feet is just as important as what you wear. If you plan to kick your opponent in the face, beach thongs probably will hurt you more than him. Wear tennis shoes, well broken-in boots, or similar shoes that will protect your feet and offer the best kicking surface. Your $300 dress loafers may not give you as much help as a decent pair of running shoes. Why ruin expensive shoes kicking some creep? If you must walk long distances in unfamiliar or downright bad territory, wear tennis shoes, carry your business shoes, and change later. Those soft tennies will help you kick hard and get out of the area much better.

Here are a few other tips for fighting in street clothes while outside the safety and comfort of your home or training room:

• Don't call attention to yourself. Try not to stand out among the locals. Start off by wearing appropriate items for wherever you plan to go. Whenever possible, dress for the neighborhood where you'll be walking. In other words, don't wear a tuxedo in the ghetto.

• Favor loose pants, shirts (or muscle shirts and tank tops if you have enough to fill them out), and light, nondescript coats.

• Stay away from those jackets that tout your favorite sports teams. In some parts of town even wearing one is an invitation to get mugged or ambushed by large groups of unfriendly sports fans who like other teams. Worse yet, these jackets sell well on the streets, and certain career hoods would fight to the death to steal yours.

• If you have time to anticipate a pending fight, take off bulky items and either drop them on the ground or use them as a blocking tool to protect yourself from body blows. This includes your sweater, jacket, umbrella, briefcase, lunch box, backpack, tool box, grocery bags, or whatever you carry that you can use to block with or swing as a weapon.

• Remove a piece of clothing like a hat, sunglasses, or a belt and wave them to distract your opponent. When he's looking at what you're holding in front of him, use the moment to punch or kick at will.

• Wear comfortable shoes that will double as kicking tools and getaway mobiles. In some cases, you may have to take off running to avoid post-fight problems with your opponent's angry pals.

Studies of crime and interviews with long-time strong-arm robbers, muggers, and thieves tell us that these people look for targets that appear out of the ordinary. If you're wearing a $1,000 suit, carrying a $500 briefcase, and sporting $200 sunglasses, you may not have a problem walking through a yacht club parking lot. But if you happen to end up in the less-fortunate side of town, you will stick out like a sore thumb. This kind of fashion statement may say "I've arrived" to the banker and lawyer set, but it also will say "I'm ready to be attacked" to those folks who make their living by using hard words and hard fists.

If you're going through a "tough times" neighborhood, better to dress like one of the locals. Any deviation on your part, any attempt to look like what they're not, is an invitation for trouble.

If you've read all of this book up until this point, you should be able to handle yourself quite well. But since discretion is the better part of your potential emergency room bill, it's far wiser to blend in with the crowd.

CHAPTER 10

The Dynamics of the Street

"You become champion by fighting one more round. When things are tough, you fight one more round."

—James J.
"Gentleman Jim" Corbett

This last chapter offers a simple philosophy: never go out looking for a streetfight, but always be the first to end it should it happen. I'll discuss some practical ways to control street confrontations, and some people, places, and potential problem situations you should try to avoid. I'll also teach you to see the world like street people do—as a potential battleground filled with predators and victims.

CONDITIONS WHITE, YELLOW, AND RED

Anytime you are out on the streets, stay ready and alert for what I call "problem people." These abnormal folks are the ones who go out of their way to make life miserable for us normal folks. They're called problem people because they *cause* problems for the people they encounter and they *create* problems for the people who have to deal with them, e.g., the police, paramedics, social service workers, and emergency room personnel.

Your encounter with one of these problem people may happen tomorrow or never. You may take the principles of this book, train with enthusiasm, and never meet up with them. Or you may put this book down and become involved in a fight for your life several hours later. You just can't predict when or where you will run across a street thug who will want to hurt you for the money in your wallet or just because he feels like doing it.

As such, anytime you leave the relative safety of your home or work place, go into "Condition Yellow." This calls for you to be visually and mentally ready for anyone who comes near you. Condition Yellow differs from Condition White, which is a position of physical unreadiness, like you might exhibit were you at home watching TV or taking a nap.

Condition White is fine for home or work, but it's totally unacceptable for walking the streets. Yet most people walk around in Condition White 24 hours a day! They seem oblivious to the dangers out there and hardly notice the streetwise attackers who see them as instant targets.

Would you walk the streets with your head in a newspaper? Would you carry on a deep conversation with a friend and never look around you? Would you park your car on a dark street just to save parking fees?

While you may not do these things, rest assured countless numbers of people who are in a permanent state of Condition White do it all the time! When they try to explain to the police what happened, they can't. A common streetfight story starts with the familiar statement, "I never saw him until it was too late. He hit me and took my money and ran off. I think he was wearing a dark colored jacket, but I'm not sure."

If you stay in Condition Yellow while on the streets, you can avoid wearing that invisible label that says "VICTIM" to every crook you pass. They certainly know who is aware and alert and who presents the easiest, softest target. They don't want to mess with people who look, walk, and act like they are in Condition Yellow. They are not interested in scrapping with people who are hard targets and look like they may kick their butts. Their muddy but practical philosophy is "Why risk fighting with someone who may pound me if I can attack some idiot who's not even looking at me?"

If you're already in Condition Yellow, it's very easy to jump to Condition Red, which is full-blown punching and kicking activity. Getting to Condition Red means you and your opponent are about to fight and you are more than ready to get in the first fight-ending strike.

It's difficult to get your brain and body up to full speed when you're in Condition White. To prove this idea, try a simple test: the next time you wake from a sound sleep, immediately jump out of bed and pretend to attack an imaginary opponent standing at your bedside. Not too easy is it? Your muscles seem tight, your brain is still a bit fuzzy, and it's hard to get your body to move quickly or correctly.

Now try the same test, except stay in Condition Yellow this time. Lie awake on your bed and move when you feel ready to deal with the threat. See the difference? Your muscles are warm and ready, your brain is up to full speed, and you can move quickly and hit hard.

KEY: This simple test should show you something important: you can defend yourself from Condition Yellow, not from Condition White. If you're out on the streets, even for a brief period of time, be ready to defend yourself. The street predators you encounter will attack without warning. You should be able to strike back without hesitation.

CREATING A SAFE DISTANCE

Now that you're in Condition Yellow, you should know how to *read* the streets and decide what looks safe and normal and what looks dangerous and abnormal. Being alert to problem people means you must gauge distances between yourself and others you pass. One of the main reasons why Condition White is so risky is that it allows people to get too close to you. Since you can't react as fast as you can act, it gives your assailant a huge head start on you.

Commit this Condition Yellow safety guide to memory and follow it closely. On a street that is *not* filled with people:

• You should visually identify anyone within 40 feet of your position.

• You should make eye contact with anyone within 20 feet of your position.

• You should verbally stop anyone who comes within 10 feet of your position.

• You should prepare to defend yourself if anyone comes within 5 feet of your position.

• You should be ready to attack anyone who blocks your path or comes within arm's length of your position.

These numbers are approximations, but they should give you an accurate guideline to help you protect yourself. Normal people don't come close to other people on the streets. They usually go about their business and keep their distance from each other. Street people, on the other hand, enjoy confrontations. They like to step into your path, call your attention to them, or make it difficult for you to get past them.

Street panhandlers, in particular, will verbally and physically confront their prey in hopes of badgering or shaming them into giving up some money. Many of these street tactics border on strong-arm robbery or extortion. Some people will give these bums money just to be "released" from their verbal "hold," like buying a toy for a crying child just to appease him, but this time with more threatening overtones.

Keep in mind that the numbers above apply to mostly empty streets, not those teeming with noontime or after-work crowds. The phrase "safety in numbers" applies in those situations, but when you are one of the only people on the streets, stay in Yellow and gauge your distances. You will have no problem justifying the defense of your life if you are walking down an empty street and some hood crosses over to meet up with you. You can be almost certain he has your money on his mind.

KEY: In some cases, a strong verbal command like, "Hey! Back off! Don't mess with me!" may be enough to scare off the average panhandler, but it might not stop the average mugger. That's why you should give a verbal command at 10 feet; you'll still have enough time to prepare your attack if he fails to stop.

THE STREET ENCOUNTER PHILOSOPHY

This book has tried to drive home the "street encounter philosophy"—never go out looking for problems with other people, but always be ready, willing, and able to finish them if need be. If you let the bad guys make the decision for you, you could be injured or dead before you get the first punch in.

All of urban life is really street theater. Street people will avoid you if you are obviously larger and in better physical and mental shape then them, you do not present an easy target, or they think you may be crazier then they are.

Use bluffs to try to talk your way out of things, act like a nut, or do something totally unexpected or crazy to make a potential attacker think *more* than twice about mixing it up with you. Try screaming wildly, throwing your arms around, or running around in circles. You'd be amazed how many street people get frightened by nutty behavior in so-called "normal" people. It can make them question their own already-twisted view of reality if someone who is "supposed" to be normal apparently loses control in front of them.

But your little street acting lesson is more than just a show. While you're acting like a certified mental patient, you can be planning your escape or your attack if the need arises.

Street people respect fitness. They know instinctively (just like animals) that the biggest of the species will be the hardest to hit and the hardest to bring down. Big muscles take up eye space in their "camera lens" eyeballs. Everywhere they look they see you. If you're in shape and relatively well-built, it makes them think it will hurt them a hell of a lot more if you hit them than if they hit you.

Whatever you say or do on the streets—from verbal threats to assuming a fighting stance—be ready to back it up with action. Walk the talk and walk it like you talk it. As the old saying about toughness goes, "Don't write checks your body can't cash." Don't waste time talking like a big-mouth. If a fight is inevitable, get in the first shot and then split when he's down.

I can't stress enough the need to keep your macho side under control, just like the scholar-warrior described in Chapter 1. Be tough, but be tough in a controlled, thoughtful way. Too much booze, showing off in front of women, and a foolish desire to save your worldly possessions can get you killed. Read the streets, see the danger zones, and get ready to vote with your feet if necessary. There's no shame in splitting if the odds greatly outweigh your success.

If there are five of them and one of you, start the foot race. If you're in shape and they're not, it can't last for more than a few blocks. Besides, just like the story of the grizzly bear chasing the two hunters, you don't have to outrun all of them, just the fastest guy. And if he's a beer-filled, lung-blown dope smoker, this won't be too hard.

Many of the problems that follow an initial street confrontation come when the "winner" stays in the area long enough for the "loser" to regroup or rearm himself with more friends, a gun, or both. The best way to survive this "second half" is not to be there when it comes around. The classic story of the bar bouncer smacking some street hood around and throwing him out in front of his friends is almost always followed by a drive-by shooting that kills him or an innocent patron leaving the bar. If you work in a place like that, be careful who you insult and who you hit as you perform your duties. If you don't have to earn a living in such locales, avoid them.

If you kick somebody's butt, especially in a social context like at a party or in a bar in front of his or your friends, rest assured he probably will come back to retaliate with some kind of weapon or more bodies. After any fight, it should suddenly be time to leave. You can safely exult over your victory back home.

Don't get caught up in someone else's problems, and never be the one who stands around bragging about a hard-fought victory. If you have to fight with some street hood, do it correctly (get in the first and only punch or kick) and leave. Don't wait for his reinforcements to come back in several cars or out from the barrel of a gun.

READING THE TERRAIN

Read people just like you would read the streets. If two guys are lingering near an Automatic Teller Machine (ATM) with no real business there, go to another location. If two guys are sitting in the parking lot of your bank, looking sweaty and glancing around all the time, go to another location. Don't engage in long conversations with obviously crazy people, transient money beggars, stolen jewelry salesmen, or anyone else who might want to do you and your wallet harm.

If you see someone lingering outside a liquor store, decide if he's a customer or a robber busy casing the place. If he's covered head to foot in poor-quality prison tattoos and wearing a long wool overcoat on a hot day, chances are he's gearing himself up to rob the store or you should you stumble into his path.

Don't get too close, don't get personally involved, and do worry about protecting your body first and your goodies second. Read body language at all times. If you come across a problem person who flexes his fists, talks to himself, and looks around a lot, he could be a former or current mental patient waiting to go off. If you're the closest "wall" for him to bounce against, he could quickly become a dangerous opponent.

Know the parts of the B.E.A.T. model (BRAIN, EYES, ABDOMEN, TESTICLES) and how to shut them down. If your enemy can't think, see, breathe, or use his crushed groin area for normal functions, he won't be too concerned about hurting you anymore. Walk around in Condition Yellow whenever you're not home and safe.

Much of your safety and survival in the urban jungle revolves around the way problem people perceive you. What is important is how they look at you, what image you give off, what kind of "force presence" you display, whether you can earn immediate respect with your build, fitness level, facial expressions, and the all-important presence of an I-don't-give-a-damn attitude. Honing this last life-saving belief to a fine degree can help you give off an "aura" that says, "I will fight you if you try to attack me, and it will hurt you badly."

Use some common sense on the streets. Don't go to places where problem people always congregate. Why put your head into the lion's mouth if you don't have to? Avoid bad-ass bars and taverns, topless nightclubs in seedy parts of town, ATMs in the wee hours of the morning, deserted streets, empty parking lots, and liquor stores or check-cashing spots in unpleasant neighborhoods. Don't pass through housing projects, large parks, or alleys unless it's absolutely necessary.

ARMED CONFLICTS

If you must go up against an knife wielder, try to judge him as quickly as humanly possible. Is he some drunk who you can knock on his ass? Or is he a trained knife fighter intent on carving you up? Remember, you can't react as fast as he can act. By the time you encounter his knife, you could already be seriously injured. Get as much space between him

THE DYNAMICS OF THE STREET

and you, and use outside barriers like coats, cars, mailboxes, fire hydrants, or other people to block his path toward you. Get away as quickly as you can.

If he is armed with a handgun, start talking fast. Tell him you're more than ready to give him what he wants and to let him be on his way. Hand over some token amount of money—a collection of ones in a bundle—and then split as he counts them out.

If you get hassled by a panhandler who *appears* to be unarmed, never take your eyes off him after you've said "no" to his request for money. These people can get highly incensed if they think you've "insulted" them by not helping out. It's quite common for a simple panhandler to quickly turn into an armed robber or a murderer by pulling out a razor, knife, or screwdriver and using it on some poor soul that didn't give him a quarter.

These problem people seem to prefer knives as the "panhandler's" weapon of choice. Knives are simple to use, quiet, efficient, cheap to get, easily concealable, and require no bullets or special training. And knives and other edged weapons are easy to ditch and recover later should the cops show up for a pleasant chat about urban crime.

Thanks to TV news and liberal social support groups, panhandlers have this benign reputation as "gentle souls down on their luck." Don't be fooled by their shuffling gait or scruffy appearance. Watch these street people carefully and give them a wide berth after you've turned them away with a simple and direct "no." And if that means turning completely around and watching them walk down the street, do it. Dropping your guard from Condition Yellow to Condition White is an easy way to get sucker-punched from behind or stabbed in the back.

HOW TO READ A CROOK LIKE A BOOK

As you eat your lunch in the park one fine day, you see a

male street person sitting on a nearby bench, rocking back and forth and talking quietly to himself. He appears to be looking down at the ground and his arms are folded tightly across his chest. He's rocking steadily and while you can't quite make out what he's saying, it sounds like he's having a two-way conversation with himself. Every few minutes, he looks up from his one-way dialogue and quickly scans the surrounding area for trouble. His eyes bolt open wide when he sees you looking back at him. He rises and quickly comes toward you . . .

You and your buddy are at the beach with some friends. You see three people standing nearby and they are arguing loudly with each other. Two of the participants are male and one is a female, who stands off to the side crying and talking incoherently. One of the males starts griping to you about the problem. It seems each man claims the woman is his girlfriend and wants the other guy to leave. Out of the corner of your eye, you see your friend talking to the other man. As he tells his story to your pal, you see him look at the other boyfriend and start to take several deep breaths, loudly exhaling each time. After three or four of these breaths, he starts to clench and unclench his hands, all the while looking at the other suitor. Then he shifts his head and neck muscles from side to side as if he were trying to loosen up . . .

You and your wife are walking through a large outdoor shopping mall. As you cross from one side to the other, you see a man walking parallel with you, but almost in the "blind spot" over your left shoulder. When you stop, he stops and when you speed up, he follows suit. He avoids making eye contact with you and is dressed in loose clothing, a ball cap, and running shoes. You also notice that your wife is carrying her purse in a rather haphazard fashion, swinging it back and forth around her wrist. As you look back over your shoulder one last time, he is already a few steps from her arm . . .

With your 20-20 hindsight vision safely stored away, take

a guess as to what might happen in each of these common street scenarios. A quick review:

Scene #1—The guy has wrapped his arms tightly around himself and is carrying on a deep conversation with said parties unknown. Scene #2—One guy is taking in large quantities of O^2 and flexing his fists. He's also trying to loosen that small tension-based kink in his neck. Scene #3—This guy is avoiding your eyes, tracking you like a fox after a rabbit, and wearing "felony flying gear."

If you guessed "Punch me, punch the other guy, and head for the hills with her purse," give yourself a gold star.

People—as I have said in these pages many times before—act just like animals. They move around like animals, think like animals, and in some cases, eat and even look like animals. If you know how to read the signs of impending danger, you can take the necessary steps to avoid injury.

Remember how the cartoons always show an angry bull pawing at the ground and snuffling his steamy breath before he charges after someone? This is known as a "preattack" stance. The human movements described in each of the three scenarios above also illustrate preattack positions.

When wild animals are put into potentially dangerous or life-threatening situations, they react by gearing themselves up to fight or scampering off in the opposite direction of their foes. Humans are no different. If you see someone shifting his position to a more bladed, sideways stance, flexing his hands and fingers, or staring at some area on your body where a punch might do some damage, look out!

Failing to read body language in time can give a crook that extra-second jump on you. This means by the time the punch is a foot away from your chops, it's probably too late.

In the first scenario in the park, you're probably dealing with a mentally ill person. This "holding it in" posture gives a good indication that the person has paranoid or delusional feelings and may be trying to talk himself into a violent confrontation with real or imaginary enemies.

In the second boyfriend-girlfriend confrontation, the one guy has lost interest in what your friend is saying to him, choosing to gird himself for a sucker punch aimed at the other boyfriend's noggin. His "target acquisition" stare, the warm-up breaths, and the flexing of hands and neck are just a way to tell you, "I'm preparing myself for a fight. I'm going to get my lungs and fighting tools tuned up and ready to go."

In the third scenario, this rip-off artist is stalking his prey just like a lion waiting in the weeds. His lack of eye contact and style of dress makes him look nondescript for the police description that will surely follow.

So what should you do when you spot these kinds of body language signals? You could start by talking to these problem people about their nonverbal behaviors. Tell them that you've noticed these movements and you already know what they're planning to do.

If you encounter potentially dangerous and emotionally disturbed people, start talking to them. Maintain a safe distance, but make sure they realize you're speaking to them and you think they may need some help. Don't ignore the signs. They may be trying to give you a warning—just like a dog growls, a cat hisses, and a snake coils up and rattles.

If you see someone clenching up, moving into a slight boxer's stance, and getting ready to fight, immediately break his chain of thought by saying, "Hey! Calm down! I can see you're upset, but just back off!"

And if you see someone who appears to be stalking you, stop dead in your tracks and look right at him. You might try pointing directly at him and saying to your wife, "Is that the guy?" Few crooks are dumb enough to stand around after you've "made" them.

Many times when you call people on their nonverbal behavior, you can catch them off guard. It can take the wind out of their sails and show them that you've already spotted their danger signs and will take action if they continue.

SOME LAST WORDS OF ADVICE AND WARNING

• Stay in Condition Yellow at all times. Have a plan of attack, defense, or retreat ready for each street situation you may have to face.

• Pay close attention to the body language of problem people you encounter, especially the movements and mannerisms of street hoods, high-profile gang members, drunks and dope users, panhandlers, and mentally ill people. How they stand, walk, and talk may tell you what they plan to do next.

• Practice "if-then" thinking at all times, e.g., "If he approaches me to panhandle, I will . . ."

• Maintain a safe distance. Cross the street, park around the block, or go to a location that has more lights, less problem people, and a safer feel to it.

• Stay sharp, both mentally and physically. Practice your fist and foot strikes constantly, and learn to think about your areas of weakness like a street hood might.

• Control your own body language during a potential streetfight situation. Show your opponent your strength, body control, and force presence.

• Breathe as slowly as you can during the crucial "go-no go" part that occurs before any streetfight situation. Controlled, careful breathing will help to lower your adrenaline level and prevent "tunnel vision" from hitting you.

• Learn to move laterally away from your attacker. Force him to chase you as he fights only forward and backward.

• Keep the attacker off-balance, both mentally and physically, whenever possible, e.g., use noise or movement distractions, quick in-and-out thrusts, and hand and foot fighting techniques he neither expects nor can defend against.

• Don't let the attacker distract you with one hand—shouting, pointing his finger, or waving his arm—while the other hand reaches for a weapon. Be ready for an assault from every angle.

• Focus your blows on your attacker's nerve sites and pressure points. A single well-placed strike can cause enough dysfunction to cripple his arms or legs long enough for you to finish the fight and leave.

• Be prepared to retreat when necessary in a high-danger situation.

• Since we plan to be devious and take our enemy by surprise, consider using

GET THE FIRST FIGHT-ENDING STRIKE IN AND YOU'LL COME OUT A WINNER.

kicks to the head before punches. Any successful head-kicking movement can be devastating and final. If you have the flexibility, the leg strength, and the grit to train correctly, you can put your opponent down and out without breaking a sweat.

• Hit harder, absorb pain if it comes, put your opponent down on the ground, and get out of the area before the guns come out.

• Pain or the sight of your blood is no indication of how badly you are hurt. You can and will survive most assault-type wounds. Only a fraction of streetfighting injuries actually are fatal. Keep going no matter how bad it looks!

• Always remember a veteran street cop's motto: God gave you hands to protect your face, a chin to protect your throat, shoulders to protect your jaw, arms to protect your body, hips to protect your groin, and finally, a brain to protect your life.